"Bobby—my dear friend. A man for all seasons who shares his gifts with us, and we are all so grateful."
—*Ann-Margret*

"From Philly to Vegas, from Wildwood to Hollywood, and from Cameo to the Copa, the Bobby Rydell story reads like an Academy Award-winning movie. Both Sinatras, Sr. and Jr., recognized Robert as the best of the boy singers of his day. He's been up and down…over and out, but still remains today at the top of his profession. You can call him a STAR. I call him my friend."
—*Sid Mark*
(Host/producer of nationally syndicated "Sounds of Sinatra")

"Bobby and I have been friends forever, and I thought I knew everything there was to know about him—until I read this wonderful book. Great insight into my friend's life. Love the book and love you Bobby."
—*James Darren*

"A true life story about the ups and downs of one of the most talented people I've known. His tell-all story is honest and revealing to his many fans around the world. As your friend for 60 years plus, I congratulate you… you're one hell of a man. Thanks for sharing your captivating life experiences. Your true friend and fan."
—*Frankie (Cheech) Avalon*

"*Teen Idol On The Rocks* is a must read for anybody who loves music. Bobby shows us that we can all come through adversity when you allow love, friendship, and music into your life. It's a wonderful book, written by a wonderful singer."
—*Steve Lawrence*

"The first 'troubadour/singer' to gain true fame was a guy named Al Jolson, nearly 100 years ago. Since then, they have come by the decade: Vallee, Columbo, Crosby, Sinatra, Como, Damone, Boone, Lawrence, Darin, and—in a different idiom—Frankie Laine, Johnnie Ray, and even Elvis Presley. To be such an artist takes more sweat, strain, intense devotion, and dedication than most people can conceive of. But Bobby Rydell is that type of artist. His name holds an honored place on the list. I've had the privilege of knowing Bob for many decades, so I'd like to say a few facts about Bob as I see him today: His voice is pure because his heart is pure; he has dedicated himself to a lifetime of developing, honing, refining, and sharpening his craft to a total state of excellence that is unparalleled in the music industry; and at the same time, he is—and always has been—a good and gentle man. I am pleased to call him friend. Hang in there Bobby!"
—*Frank Sinatra, Jr.*

"I've known Bobby Ridarelli forever, going back to the Paul Whiteman show, long before he became a superstar. There was no doubt in my mind back then that it would happen. He had that rare talent, not only as a singer and musician, but also in his natural flair for comedy. It would be just a matter of time. I've seen him go through the good years, the rough years, the healthy years, and there is one thing you can say about Bobby: He is truly a survivor. In this book you'll hear firsthand about how it all happened. Bobby knows that what keeps us going in show business is the audience, and his ability to connect with his audience is second to none."
—*Jerry Blavat (The Geator with the Heator)*

"It's like Bobby is sitting next to you telling his story. Inspirational, vivid, spirited, and as we all expected, heartwarming. He was, and will always be, family. Read it and smile."
—*Cousin Brucie Morrow (Broadcaster, Sirius XM)*

"The talent of Bobby Darin and Bobby Rydell are absolute equals in my mind, with an edge toward Rydell. I've worked with a lot of comedic talent throughout my career, and there's no one funnier than Bobby. His staying power is incredible! When I watch him on stage, I'm in awe. I tried singing like him once and I was in traction for two months. It is always an honor to be on the same stage with him."
—*Fabian Forte*

"For the past six decades, Bobby has continued to perform his great hits with the same energy and youthful sounding voice. But at this stage of his life, the love of his craft becomes more apparent as he displays his interpretive skills singing the Great American Songbook. His musicality has always been evident, but now a sense of wisdom and zest for life shines through, whether he's swinging a standard or caressing the lyrics of a ballad. I've always been a fan, but more importantly, I'm proud to have him as a pal."
—Dennis Bono
(The Dennis Bono Show, Live from South
Point Casino, Las Vegas, Nevada)

"I remember first meeting Bobby Rydell on the *Caravan of Stars* tour—upbeat guy, electrifying, uplifting, filled the room with energy and joy. Then I heard him sing!!! Crazy good. Man, this guy's in the pocket like nobody else—definitely a great rhythm singer. I said I could be this guy's friend for sure. Well, six decades later, I can say we have never had an argument. I attribute that to him. I still love his company; he's still got it."
—Dion DiMucci

"I first met Bobby back in 1960 and I was taken by his kindness and talent. His new book tells you who he really is and covers his personal trials and triumphs, his ups and downs, and his victories and failures. It's a great read!"
— "Little Anthony" Gourdine
(of Little Anthony and the Imperials)

BOBBY RYDELL
Teen Idol On The Rocks
A Tale of Second Chances

WITH ALLAN SLUTSKY

Published by
Doctor Licks Publishing
Cherry Hill, NJ 08002

ISBN: 978-0-9973851-0-6
eISBN: 978-0-9973851-1-3

Printed in the United States of America

Cover and Interior Design: GKS Creative

Back Cover Photo: Clay Hereth

Back Cover Synopsis: Susan Whitall

Book Production and Project Management: The Cadence Group

Editing Credits: Ruth Fecych (principal editor) and Joanne Slutsky,
Sue Whitall, Linda J. Hoffman (Ridarelli), Linda Ferrino (Hoffman),
Jim Gorecki, Sam Slutsky, Rachel Slutsky, and Craig Weiland
helped with additional editing.

All photos are from the private collections of Bobby Rydell and Linda Ferrino
(Hoffman), except for the photo on page 153 which came from Joe Nero.
Best efforts were made to find the original photographers on the remaining
five-decades-old photos.

Library of Congress Information is on file with the Publisher.

In memory of:

Camille Ridarelli
Adrio "Ott" Ridarelli
and Julia

Dedicated to the two Lindas in my life:

Linda J. Hoffman (Ridarelli)
and Linda Ferrino (Hoffman)

TABLE OF CONTENTS

FOREWORD

We call them *shade pullers*. In the vernacular of musicians in the showroom-pit orchestra world, that's an apt description of the type of stars who draw a line of demarcation—a no-go zone—between themselves and the people who bring their musical acts to life.

Stories about them abound in the Philadelphia-Atlantic City musicians' community. There was one singer, a real diva, who ordered her management to issue a behind-the-curtains edict that "musicians and stage-hands were not permitted to make eye-contact with their artist in any backstage area of the theater." And you can just imagine the love we felt for a certain octogenarian comedian and star of film and TV who pulled this classy stunt: After a saxophonist in the house band had the audacity to say to him, "Great show tonight," he quickly exited the stage, and while making his way to the safety and exclusivity of his dressing room, remarked to his manager, "I thought I told you to keep those goddamn musicians away from me."

Bobby Rydell is the antithesis of a *shade puller*. In fact, he's usually the guy who *initiates* interactions with musicians, sound and light crew, and basically anyone else within earshot. I learned this in 1992 on the first night of a three-month run of *American Bandstand: A Musical Happening* at Atlantic City's Tropicana Casino.

When I was a kid in the early '60s, it was impossible to go more than a few weeks without seeing Bobby's face pop up on any one of a dozen TV variety and talk shows. How many times an hour did WIBG play "Volare" during the summer of 1960? Ten? Twelve? Maybe not, but it sure seemed that way. And if you walked the boardwalk in Atlantic City, all paths eventually led to one of his iconic performances at Steel Pier. Almost everyone in Philadelphia felt like they knew Bobby Rydell on a first-name basis—even if they really didn't. He was the personification of the kid down the block.

The Trop gig was the first time I met him in person, let alone had the opportunity to play guitar on one of his shows. My first sight of Bobby, at the show's initial rehearsal, was not of him standing aloofly in the wings, talking with his manager, the show's producer, or the Tropicana's director of entertainment; he was hanging out with the horn section, laughing his ass off while trading musicians' war stories. Throughout the run, it was rare not to see him in our dressing room before each show sharing a taste from a bottle, telling a particularly filthy joke, lamenting about the previous night's baseball game, or asking someone about a member of their family.

He'd just turned fifty, but seemed more like a seventeen-year-old kid hanging on a South Philly street corner with his boys. His youthful spirit and love of performing were infectious, and made everyone in the orchestra want to bring their "A" game to each show. It reminded me of the way Vince Lombardi, or any great coach, inspires his team to give their all and want to play for them.

A few weeks after the Trop show's summer-long run came to an end, I was thrilled and honored when Bobby asked me to arrange and produce an album for him. I was thrilled once again, and also flabbergasted, when I watched him knock off the vocals on almost every track in just a single take. There were very few (if any) punch-ins for him; the vocals I heard—traveling from his diaphragm, to his mouth, to the microphone, and finally, to the rotating reels of two-inch magnetic tape—were right in the pocket. Phrasing, time, pitch—they were all there. All I could do was shrug my shoulders and say, "Uhh . . . I guess we'll move on to the next song." It was obvious to everyone in the recording studio's control booth that the guy at the mic was a consummate pro who had stored up a lifetime of show biz and musical lessons during his long career.

Yet all of these qualities take a backseat to Bobby's endurance and toughness. He's weathered a lot of storms during his lifetime: changing musical trends and tastes, life-threatening health issues, struggles with the bottle, and lifelong battles with other internal demons. Yet, through it all, he emerged as someone loyal to a fault to his friends, and fiercely in love with the life he's been given. Only one word can adequately describe him: he's a survivor. For the sake of his legions of friends and fans, I hope this Golden Boy continues to survive for years to come.

Allan Slutsky

February 20, 2016

♩ INTRO & VAMP

I f it hadn't been for the antiseptic smell of the floors and walls, the corridor I was traveling down would have been unremarkable. I could have easily mistaken it for a service hallway leading to a showroom at the Sahara, the Sands, the Golden Nugget, or any one of the dozens of casinos I'd sung at throughout my career. But this was no ordinary walk toward a spotlight. I was en route to the biggest and most challenging performance of my life. I wasn't walking; I was flat on my back on a hospital gurney, being wheeled into an operating room for double organ transplant surgery.

I was as calm and focused as I had ever been. It was spooky. There was no panic, no second guessing, and most of all, none of that whiny, *"I used to be the biggest teen idol in America, I sold over 25 million records, met with kings, queens and presidents, sang for millions of adoring fans at thousands of concerts across the world . . . so how the hell did I get here?"* kind of crap. I had no right to feel sorry for myself. I knew damn well how I had gotten where I was: Decades of drinking had ravaged my body and wrecked my liver and kidneys. I had no one to blame but yours truly.

A few days before, my doctors had told me I wouldn't live out the week. And then a Hail Mary pass arrived out of nowhere. Someone else's tragic death had provided me with a second chance at life and salvation. A liver and kidney had turned up that were the match the medical staff at Thomas Jefferson University Hospital had been searching for.

I figured I had nothing to lose. I'd never had stage fright in my entire career so I sure wasn't going to start having it now. I could read the cards. It was simple: I was either going to make it through this surgery or I wasn't. Until that point came, I still had business to conduct. There was one date remaining on my tour schedule: I was supposed to perform on a cruise ship sailing the Caribbean in three months. I thought it over, and being a gambling man, decided to bet on me. Just as I was wheeled into the operating theater, I smiled at my wife, Linda, gently squeezed her hand and said, "I'm gonna make that cruise."

TIMPANI ROLL & VAMP

"Yo Bobby, I got your biography right hee-ah!"
(Cymbal crash)

That, my friends, is a dead-on caricature of the bullshit, but fun-loving image of South Philly that's evolved over the last few decades. Maybe it grew out of Sylvester Stallone's *Rocky* movies or all those over-the-top cheesesteak and soft pretzel ads; maybe not. But, there's no denying that crotch-grabbing *gavones* like the wannabe literary critic who just delivered the aforementioned line do presently exist in my old neighborhood.

Now mind you, I'm sure his good wishes would have been delivered with great respect and affection. You see, I've been fortunate enough to have earned that kind of street corner reverence from my hometown over the years. In fact, there's a plaque on Broad Street's *Walk of Fame* with my name on it, and even a street at 11th and Moyamensing called *Bobby Rydell Boulevard.*

But in 1942, when my story starts, that little slice of Heaven bore very little resemblance to South Philly's current image. The neighborhood of my youth was a place where no one ever felt the need to lock their doors. Kids played halfball, pimpleball, and Buck Buck in the streets, while old men sat on their front steps with transistor radios glued to their ears, ever hopeful that the perennially pathetic Phillies might actually win a World Series before they died. George's Ice Cream Parlor, the ultimate hangout for teenagers, was just up the street, and so were all your friends. Everyone lived within a few blocks of each other.

Periodically, Italian street parades marched up Broad Street or in front of parish churches, with bands playing mazurkas, tarantellas and other Italian favorites. When you entered just about any house before supper, the sweet, pungent aroma of marinara cooking on the stove overwhelmed you. By the way, "mah-rree-nah-rrah" is the word—*not* sauce, *not* gravy. And then those smells . . . *Oh, Mar-rone!! (Oh, Madonna Mia* in non-South Philly Italian*)*. Every night, when dinner time arrived, a neighborhood oratorio of high-pitched mothers' voices called their kids in to eat. And as a final reward every night, I got to fall asleep with the mouth-watering scent of freshly baked bread drifting through my bedroom window from Giuffre's Bakery around the corner. What a place to grow up!

You'd be smiling too if you lived in South Philly back in the day.

With my parents at age 1.

VERSE 1

The two surnames I inherited when I came into this world on April 26th, 1942 were not a great match. *Ridarelli* translates from Italian to English as "laughter," something that's no doubt been an essential element of both my personality and my professional career. Now, *Sapienza*? That one doesn't fit quite as well. It translates as "wisdom," which flies in the face of some of the questionable life choices I've made over the past seven decades.

Nevertheless, for better or worse, that was the genealogy I was stuck with when my parents named me Robert Louis Ridarelli and brought me home from the Jewish Hospital (now known as Einstein Medical Center) in the Olney section of Philadelphia. My dad's name was Adrio Ridarelli, but everyone called him "Al" or "Ott" after his favorite baseball player, New York Giants' slugger Mel Ott. Mom was just plain old Jennie, and home was a red brick row house at 2423 South 11th Street, that was virtually indistinguishable from every other house on the block. It belonged to my mom's parents, Antonio and Lena Sapienza, who lived with us—or I should say, we lived with them.

Our house had four bedrooms. My grandparents' room looked out over the backyard and my parents' bedroom faced 11th Street. You'd figure a four-bedroom house would leave plenty of room for five people, but the rooms were small, and there was only one bathroom—which my grandfather usually monopolized. When I finally got in there, I often noticed his false teeth with those pinkish, artificial gums soaking in a glass of water on top of the sink. Out of curiosity I tried them on one time. I couldn't figure out how they fit so I gave up and settled for the teeth I already had.

And as for air conditioning . . . What? Are you kiddin' me? No one in the neighborhood had air conditioners back then. We just turned on a fan, opened all the windows and doors and made do with whatever breeze we could generate. It wasn't that bad, and no one knew better anyway. Besides, most of my summers were spent at my grandmother's boarding house at 232 East Montgomery Avenue in the ocean-cooled climate of Wildwood, New Jersey. Our immediate family excluded, a hundred bucks a week got you food, room and board, and as much salt air as you wanted.

With names like Ridarelli and Sapienza, an obvious assumption would be that Italian was the primary language in our house, but it wasn't so. The only time I ever heard Italian spoken at home was when my grandparents had the occasional spat and didn't want me to know what was going on. Culturally, though, we were as Italian as it gets, particularly when it came to food, family, holidays, traditions, and the predictable roster of South Philly Italian slang words like *stunod, agita,* and *gabagool.* Most of all, there was a deep, unspoken sense of pride in the family heritage going back to the old country. My dad's parents came from a working class region of Italy known as Marche'. Mom's side of the family was from Abruzzi.

The division of labor in our house was set pretty much from the beginning: My dad left the house five days a week to operate a punch press at the Electro-Nite Carbon Company in the Holmesburg section of Philadelphia; Mom was a professional shopper and occasional housewife seven days a week; my grandmother was the world's greatest Italian cook, and my grandfather was a retiree whose principal joy—besides his family—was tending to his prized fig tree in our backyard. My job was to entertain and play and sing music.

From what my parents told me, that pursuit had begun in the crib, where they could hear me humming simple melodies. My father was drafted into the army in 1945 and went overseas with the troops that served under General Eisenhower after the war. The letters he and my mother wrote to each other revealed their growing awareness that their baby boy might have already chosen his lifetime profession. "The baby's always singing," Mom wrote my father. "Who knows? Maybe we'll have a star in the family one day," my dad wrote back. By the age of three, I took over my grandmother's pots, pans, and

Left - In the kitchen with the world's greatest cook—Grandmom Lena.
Right - Grandpop Tony and me on our front steps.

cooking utensils and turned them into my first drum set. I tried to imitate anything I heard on the radio or my dad's record player, and when we got our first TV set some years later, I'd pick up on the mannerisms of the singers, drummers, comedians and actors I watched on the early variety shows.

Despite getting off to a running start with my musical and show biz beginnings, I still managed to be a normal kid. The enticements of my South Philadelphia neighborhood were too strong to ignore. Some of the credit has to go to my next-door neighbor, Lou Cioci. The two of us were lifetime buddies from infancy and became inseparable. We did everything together, particularly when it came to television. Lou's parents owned one of the first TVs in the neighborhood and we were hooked. Lou loved cowboy shows, but we were both fans of puppet shows like *Pinhead & Houdini* and *Willie the Worm,* especially the cartoons that ran in between the puppets' skits.

Like me, Lou wasn't particularly religious, but we both wound up at Epiphany grade school at 11th and Jackson. If you were a South Philly Italian kid living within the boundaries of Epiphany Parish, that's where you went. I was never a great student. If you'd force me to come up with a fond memory from my grade school experience, well . . . let's put it this way: My favorite moments at Epiphany were when I got to leave class because a nun asked me to take the blackboard erasers out on the fire escape and clap them together to clean off the chalk dust.

The nuns separated Lou and me in first grade and put us in different classes. I cried like crazy. We finally were reunited in the fifth grade when both of us became safeties. Now *this* was important stuff! We were very proud of our official patrol belts and badges, because they gave us the authority to hold kids back at the traffic crossings and tell them when to stop and go. I took this new position very seriously. Too bad I didn't treat school the same way.

Now, I do treasure the times I spent hanging out with my school friends, most of whom were Italians—guys with names like Joe Priori, Val Troiano, two other kids nicknamed "Spider" and "Stilt," and finally, Anthony "The Animal" DeAmbra and Sebastian "Bo" Morano. Bo, the Animal and Lou Cioci were our crowd's tough guys. Me? I was so skinny, if someone punched me in the chest, their fist might come out of the other side of my body. When Bo, the Animal, or Lou got into a fight, I proudly held their school bags.

Maybe I'm making my old neighborhood sound like an Italian version of *Boyz 'N The Hood*, but the fights were kept to a minimum. Everyone usually got along. Because of the common decency of the people in our neighborhood, we were all able to enjoy a wealth of childhood experiences in a very small, confined area. Everyone either joined the local Boy Scouts (Troop 26) or the 13th Street Boys Club, where we played pool and sparred in their boxing ring. If you wanted to play stickball, you went to Jenks schoolyard (also on 13th Street) and drew a strike zone on the school's brick walls with a piece of chalk.

Few of us ever went past Broad Street or much farther east than 8th or 9th Streets. The homemade scooters that we built out of orange crates and roller skate wheels weren't really suitable for long-distance travel, so we stayed close to home. Until I went to high school, 15th Street and beyond might as well have been Mongolia; it was totally foreign territory.

The few times I ventured out of my neighborhood comfort zone was when I walked six blocks to Chadwick Street to visit the candy store owned by my father's parents, Tony and Maria, or if some of my friends and I went to Oregon Avenue to play football. (The ball was usually a rolled-up newspaper with string tied around it.)

Every kid's favorite activity took place on Saturdays, when we descended en masse upon the Colonial Theater at 10th and Moyamensing. From 10:00 a.m. until 6:00 p.m., we watched four serials—usually *Captain Marvel, Wild Bill Hickok, Roy Rogers,* and *Hopalong Cassidy*—and then a few dozen cartoons. Decked out in our cowboy boots, hats, and holstered guns, we'd spend the afternoons imitating the heroes we saw on the screen. It was a raucous affair, but the parents all loved it because we were safe and they were able to enjoy some time to themselves.

By the age of ten, the allure of the Wild West finally wore off and we replaced it with a more harmful fixation: we all started smoking. We'd sit on someone's steps playing Bill Haley, Fats Domino, and Elvis records and smoke Lucky Strikes. I fainted after my first big puff. You'd figure anyone with a brain would say, "This shit is no good for you," but not us. The immediate coolness factor far outweighed any future health concerns.

Lucky Strikes weren't the only things we started lighting at the age of 10. Candles were now added to our repertoire, when some of my friends and I became altar boys at Epiphany Parish's church. My experience might have only lasted a few times, but because Sister San Gabriel loved the way my mother dressed me for the services (with Mom, everything had to be perfect), I remained an altar boy until I was almost fifteen. My very first mass was with Joe Priori. The assignment was simple: *book* or *bell.* You carried one or the other. The left side of the altar was book, the right side was bell. Joe chose bell, I chose book. Maybe I shouldn't have; I dropped it, which got me slapped around by Father Gilooley after the service.

I was a lot happier when he was succeeded by Father Tinsel. *He* was cool! Whenever he had to turn toward the congregation, he'd do a military about-face. We also knew he cared

With my classmates at Epiphany Parish's grade school.
Don't strain your eyes; I'm just below the halfway point and
slightly to the right of center, wearing a dark sport coat and a tie.

about us as people, as opposed to just being necessary cogs in the Mass' rituals. Father Tinsel would take me and the other altar boys on trips to Willow Grove Amusement Park and to St. Charles Seminary, where we got to use their indoor track and athletic equipment. This was a big deal for kids who were used to playing out on the streets all the time.

I usually did my altar boy thing Monday through Friday at the 9:00 a.m. masses, and occasionally I also served at funerals and weddings. I always got a kick out of the old ladies at the funerals. Dressed completely in black, they were basically professional mourners whose mission was to wail and lament:

"Gesù Cristo, O Dio mio, é morto" ("Jesus, Christ, Oh my God, someone has died.") My buddies and I liked the weddings a lot better because we could make some money. The best man usually handed out tips. If it was $5.00, we were content and appreciative. If the guy was cheap and only gave us a buck or two, we'd somehow find a way to "accidentally" step on the bride's train. At the end of the service, we'd head over to the pizza place on 11th and Tree Street and get brick oven Sicilian tomato pie for ten cents a slice. The lines stretched down the entire block, but believe me, it was worth the wait.

Most of the nuns at Epiphany Parish school were tough. If you got caught chewing gum, missing mass or talking in class when you weren't supposed to, they'd whack your behind or the palm of your hand with a wooden pointer or sometimes a yardstick. Lemme tell you, they didn't pull their punches; when they punished you, it hurt like hell. I was a pretty good kid so they didn't pick on me too much, although there was one episode when I received the wrath of the rod. I had some blue pajamas that I used to wear a lot, along with a towel with a big red "S" drawn on it that I used as my cape. One day, a classroom nun asked me, "Who is the greatest power in the world?" My classmates loved it when I answered "Superman," but the nun was not amused. I had trouble sitting down the rest of the day.

In the late '40s and early '50s, the landscape of South Philly was dotted with dozens of small bars and clubs that had names like the RDA, the "24," and the Erie Social Club, most of which featured musical trios or quartets as their house bands. Before I'd even reached the ripe old age of seven, my dad started taking me around to these venues and asking the club owners if I could sit in with the band. I'd get up in front of fifty to seventy-five people, sing a few songs, and do my imitations of famous singers and actors. Frank Fontaine's Crazy Guggenheim routine from the old *Jackie Gleason Show* was the highlight of my act. It always went over like gangbusters. As young as I was, the effect I had on the audiences was not lost on me. "All I gotta do is perform stuff like this, maybe sing a few tunes and everyone applauds?" I thought. "Gee, that's kinda nice."

By the time I was ten, I was a battle-hardened veteran of the circuit, which my dad had expanded to include clubs down at the shore like Eddie Suez's Club Avalon (later renamed Cozy Morley's) in Wildwood. I even acquired my own set of charts to hand out to the house bands. After a few years of being at the mercy of whatever repertoire the clubs' musicians knew, my Dad paid a local pianist named Michael Francis to write out some arrangements for me—tunes like "I'm Gonna Live Till I Die" and other similar standards.

There is no doubt in my mind that my father was the most influential figure in my life as a kid, and throughout the rest of my life. He was a funky, South Philly kinda street guy. Handsome and vibrant, he lived life to the fullest. Breakfast was usually coffee with a shot of whiskey, into which he dunked a piece of bread, a unique component of an otherwise typical '40s South Philly diet that—by today's health standards—would

At a club doing my Frank Fontaine-Crazy Guggenheim imitation.

Performing at Eddie Suez's Club Avalon in Wildwood at age 10. (Standing in the background on the stage is my future conductor, Rocky Valentine.)

be a recipe for a major coronary attack. On top of all that, he chain smoked. None of Dad's vices could dull his deep passion for music though. It was evident in the intoxicating musical atmosphere he created around the house. He'd play popular and big band music of the '40s and '50s—Mario Lanza, Bing Crosby, Sinatra, and the other great singers of that era—and eventually, Elvis, the Everly Brothers, and numerous other rock and roll pioneers worked their way into my dad's in-house mix.

Dad never behaved like a stereotypical stage parent. He never forced me to practice eight hours a day or embarrassed me with subterfuge and stab-all-competition-in-the-back shenanigans at talent shows. Dad was easygoing, eternally positive and always made it fun, both for himself and me. He was an enabler, but in a good way. He recognized not only the talent I exhibited at a young age, but also the love I had for performing and making music. Simply put, he took it upon himself to

On the Boardwalk in Wildwood, New Jersey with my parents.

encourage me and be my traveling buddy on the road I seemed to be following—wherever it might lead.

I was a very lucky kid to have a father like that. My mother? She just didn't get it. Mom was completely unsupportive of both of us. "Where you going with all of this?" she would frequently ask my dad. "The kid's got talent, Jennie!" he would say defensively, to which Mom would always respond, "Of course you're gonna say that. You're his father."

Thankfully, the wet blanket my mother was throwing on my dad's efforts had no effect on him. In fact, he stepped up the pace by exposing me to an increasingly wider range of music, both on the radio and at live concerts. The Earle Theater at 11th and Market Street was where all that stimulation came to life for me. There, faces were attached to the voices and instruments I'd been listening to on the radio. One of the first faces I saw at the Earle belonged to the legendary, big-band era drummer, Gene Krupa. He was playing with the "King of Swing," jazz clarinetist, Benny Goodman. I was mesmerized by the excitement that rippled through the audience every time Krupa tore into a solo. During the applause, I tugged on my father's shirtsleeve and said, "I don't know who that man is, Daddy, but I want to be like him."

Several years later, my dad took me to see another star at the Earle who had the same "I want to be like him" effect on me. This time, it was much more prophetic. Johnnie Ray was a singer who many music historians consider to be the first teen idol of the rock and roll era. The night I saw him, he was riding a huge wave of success following the release of his signature No. 1 hit "Cry." (Its "B" side, "The Little White Cloud That Cried," was right behind it, reaching No. 2 on the U.S. pop charts.)

If you guessed that crying was a big part of Johnnie Ray's act, you guessed right. He wasn't dubbed "The Prince of Wails," "The Nabob of Sob," and "Mr. Emotion" for nothing. During his stage show, he would pull his hair, grimace in pain, fall down on the floor, and just flat out weep. And then—almost on cue—the helplessly seduced girls in the audience started screaming hysterically. Now I *really* knew why I wanted to be like him.

I don't want to give you the impression that the only topics of discussion between my dad and me were music and show biz. There was still plenty of time for other typical father and son activities, especially baseball. We'd often play catch, and being a die-hard Athletics fan (when they were still in Philadelphia), Dad would take me to Shibe Park to see them play. At a game against the Detroit Tigers, I screamed myself hoarse pleading with A's shortstop Eddie Joost to hit a home run. "Hit it over the wall, Eddie, hit it over the wall!" I shouted every time he came to bat. And wouldn't you know it, in his last at-bat, he crushed one. No one could tell me that he hadn't hit the homer just for me.

Yet somehow, the non-musical pursuits inevitably surrendered to the musical ones. Sometimes it was by conscious design; at others, it was a result of random outside events. One day in 1952, my dad heard that auditions were being held for *Paul Whiteman's TV Teen Club*. It was a local kids' talent show broadcast once a week from WFIL-TV's studios at 46th and Market. Eventually, it also aired on ABC's radio network. With three or four years of club performances and a sizable repertoire of songs and skits under my belt, I had a significant advantage over the other teen prospects.

Dad took me down to the studio and I mimicked a Sammy Davis Jr. routine in which he sang "Because of You" as if he were imitating Edward G. Robinson, James Cagney, Jerry Lewis, Jimmy Stewart, and a few other famous actors. I was only ten or eleven—not quite a teen as *TV Teen Club* would seem to imply—but I won the contest and landed a continuing role that lasted until the show was cancelled in 1954. The role wasn't the only thing I won. The top prize also included a TV set, an RCA Victor record player with a hefty collection of 45s, and a supply of Tootsie Rolls from the show's sponsor, which was big enough to rot out the teeth of half the kids in South Philly. Not a bad haul for a day's work.

Paul Whiteman was a larger-than-life figure, standing well over six feet and weighing more than three hundred pounds. He routinely dressed in loud, flashy shirts and sport coats and tried to relate to the teenagers in his TV audience by dropping—what he thought—were hip phrases of the day like, "Real gone, man!" Even if the kids thought that was a cool thing to say, Paul's hipness factor always dropped at the end of every show when he signed off with, "Well, that just about slaps the cap on the old milk."

He may sound corny and clownish, but if I knew then what I learned in later years, I would have been in complete awe of my new boss. A celebrated big band and symphonic orchestra leader from the '20s through the '40s, Paul was dubbed "The King of Jazz" in his early days. In 1924, he commissioned George Gershwin to write and *perform* "Rhapsody In Blue" in its world debut with him and his orchestra at New York's Aeolian Hall. Several decades later, musical giants like Duke Ellington, Gil Evans, and others still held him in the highest regard. He had worked with everyone and done it all: movies, network TV shows, and concerts all over the world. As to how the hell he wound up hosting a kids' show while in his early 60s I have no idea, but when you were around him, you could instantly tell that he clearly enjoyed what he was doing. Maybe after decades of the constant pressure that came with performing very demanding music, he just wanted to do some light lifting and have some fun.

Aside from the experience I gained on the show, my stint with the *TV Teen Club* was notable because it was the first time I used my Bobby Rydell stage name. As one story goes, Pops Whiteman couldn't pronounce Ridarelli so he shortened it to Rydell. Total bullshit. Another tale credited a nun from Epiphany's grade school, who also found my last name to be a tongue-twister. Bullshit again. *My dad* came up with the name. Neither of us looked at it as some major, life-changing decision, but it was. That spur-of-the-moment editing of our family name put an indelible stamp on my public image that is currently in its sixth decade.

"TV Teen Club" host, Paul Whiteman (center) in the early '50s. Pianist (and future head of Cameo-Parkway records) Bernie Lowe is second from the left in the dark suit.

CHORUS 1

When I hit my teens in the mid-'50s, life was very simple and stable. There were aspects of Philadelphia life you could always count on: our politicians—regardless of party—were completely corrupt, local restaurants and bars were down for the count on Sundays due to the city's restrictive blue laws, and South Philly was the place to be if you were looking for cute girls. There was no shortage of them on the streets of my little four-by-four block world. Back then, I was four or five years away from having my first hit record and the advantages that came with it. I had to chase after girls and risk rejection just like all the other Joe Shmoes out there.

Jenks schoolyard was where you went to make out if you were lucky enough to entice one of the local girls to accompany you there after dark. If you just wanted to check out the local talent and flirt, you couldn't beat George's Ice Cream

BANNIE   ANTHONY   CARMELA   LOUIE   CAROL   JOEY   CARDL   Bobby
CIOCI   PRIORI

See what I mean about cute South Philly girls? That's me
on the far right hanging out with some neighborhood friends.

Parlor. I met my first official date there—a girl named Carol
Gibson, who—in a sign of things to come—became a regular
cast dancer on *American Bandstand*. Date No. 2 (and my first
crush and pubescent fantasy) was a busty girl named Anna
who lived two blocks away. Guys in the neighborhood used
to call her "Big Tit Annie." Never to her face, mind you; we
weren't cruel. It was just inside talk among a bunch of horny
boys overwhelmed by the sight of a pin-up model's chest on a
girl who was barely a teenager. There were other girls too, but
no one really caught my eye until a neighbor named Mickey
introduced me to a friend of hers one night. I was hanging out
on her steps spinning 45s on a portable record player. The girl's
name was Camille Carmella Quattrone. Quite a mouthful to
pronounce, don't ya think? But that and every other concern

disappeared as soon as I saw her smile—a smile that could melt your heart and turn the night into day. All of that, and Camille lived just around the corner on 10th Street between Moyamensing and Porter? What more could I have asked for?

Years later, Camille told me she was in love with me before we'd even met. She went to Saint Maria Goretti High School on 10th Street. I wasn't as geographically fortunate. At that point, I was in high school at Bishop Neumann, which was located several miles away at 26th and Moore. Apparently, Camille used to hang out on the street in the mornings just to see me get on the trolley I took to school. I had no idea any of this was going on. I never noticed her. Camille was just biding her time though, believing we'd eventually meet. Once we did, she and I quickly became inseparable.

But the "we" that became inseparable was not a duo. It would always be a trio: Camille, me, and my music. And she had to make peace with that right from the beginning. That meant settling for the free time I had to spend with her when I wasn't playing clubs, practicing, or taking voice and drum lessons. Both of those studies shared the same fate, lasting only a few years. When I was eleven, South Philly vocal coach Artie Singer took me under his wing for a few years, but eventually told me to come back after my voice changed. When it did change, so did my focus; *now* I wanted to study the drums.

I'd abandoned my grandmother's pots and pans for a real set of drums when I was six or seven. My dad had gone to a pawn shop and returned home with a cheap set of metallic red sparkle drums by a company called Revere. The set's construction and sound quality weren't great, but it was good enough to pound on in our basement, when I played along with recordings of Krupa, Glen Miller, Artie Shaw, the Dorsey Brothers, and all my other big band heroes. By this time, Lou Cioci had his own musical obsession going with a trumpet. Whenever we played together, the two of us drove everyone nuts in the neighboring row homes. I knew I was good, but I also knew I needed to work on my rudiments and technique to get out of the basement.

Like Artie Singer for vocalists, Sam D'Amico was the guy everyone in the neighborhood went to when they wanted to learn how to play drums. I learned a lot from him, but after a year and a half, he told me, "Bobby, I can't teach you no more. I've shown you everything I know. You should go to New York and study with Sam Ulano."

Part of me wishes I had taken Sam D'Amico's suggestion. Sam Ulano was the master—the dean of drum teachers up in New York. But I just wanted to get out and start gigging. Even before I started with Sam D'Amico, I could already play. I was blessed with a good sense of time and I knew all the different rhythms and styles: cha-cha, bossa nova, swing, and just about any other groove I needed to be a professional drummer. But I could never explain what I was playing; I could just do it.

Remember when I was complaining earlier about how tough the nuns were in my parish? They were minor leaguers compared to the aggressive priests my friends and I encountered in high school. In today's politically correct climate, you'd never get away with the things they did to misbehaving students back then. Prior to high school, I rarely had to deal with them outside of Mass because the lower grades were taught exclusively by nuns. But at Bishop Neumann, the teachers were all laymen or Jesuit priests. The worst of them was a priest we called "Football Head," because of the odd shape of his skull. He caught a buddy of mine passing around a picture of his girlfriend during class and punched him in the stomach. When my friend doubled over in pain, Football Head knee'd him in the face. My friend staggered around for the next five minutes as if he'd been blind-sided by a car when he was crossing the street. If a teacher did that today, he'd be arrested, would probably do some jail time, and would definitely be hit with a civil suit.

In spite of their often over-the-top behavior, not all the blame should be aimed at my teachers. Technically, a lot of my friends and I may have been altar or choir boys, but outside of Mass, we tried to get away with everything we could. If a priest or layman showed any weakness, we had him; he was ours.

One of our teachers was named Mr. Sepolla. He taught biology and was as nice a guy as you'd ever meet. Naturally, we tormented him and drove him crazy. My friends and I took over the class. When Mr. Sepolla gave us a test, we'd pull out our textbooks right in front of his eyes and dare him to say something while we looked for the answers. If he complimented one of us on the way we dressed or on a recent haircut, one of the guys would tell him, "That's how much you fuckin' know." He was really a poor soul. It's a wonder he didn't wind up at Byberry (Philadelphia's psychiatric hospital, or the "nuthouse" as we used to say) after the abuse we heaped on him.

Father Koob, our principal, singled me out as the ringleader behind all this incorrigible behavior and gave me six weeks detention. He couldn't have been more wrong. I didn't have leadership skills. I was a follower. The guy who ruled the roost with me and my new set of friends in high school was Freddy Fantazzi. He was our *Don,* and Carlo Gerace and Al Nardi were his soldiers—his *capos.* Freddy was charismatic and tough as nails. After I joined the school swim team, he would bust my balls and say, "Here comes Johnny Weissmuller." I'd just smile and take it. If Freddy told you, "Hey, I don't want you to doo dat no more," you just immediately stopped doo-ing "dat," or whatever it was you were doing. None of us ever challenged him. He was the law. This was my first taste of the Cosa Nostra.

I was glad for the protection of hanging with such an intimidating crowd. The last thing I needed was to get in a fight, yet one time I did. I played timpani and snare drum in Bishop Neumann's symphony orchestra, and I was also Sergeant of the drums in the marching band. At a musical competition against Monsignor Bonner, Roman Catholic and a few other Philadelphia parochial schools, I got into an argument with one of the other drummers, and he smacked me in the face. He was a dorky-looking kid. I fought back and landed one good punch. That's all it took. Like a baseball rhubarb, it was over almost before it started. (By the way, Monsignor Bonner's marching band smoked us. They had six tubas. "B-O-N-N-E-R, BONNER!!!" What are 'ya gonna do against an advantage like that?)

Anyway, it was a good thing the fight went nowhere because I had to protect my hairdo. All the guys in my neighborhood had a sense of style, especially when it came to our haircuts. Everyone had either a duck's ass or a pompadour. I opted for the pompadour, and I gotta tell ya, it was a *world-class* one. I could walk through a wind tunnel and not a single hair follicle would move because of all the Spray Net I put on it. My pompadour was so hard, I could barely comb it, and if I had tried, all the teeth in the comb would have broken off. I had no idea just how large a role that pompadour would play a few years down the road.

There's a common misconception among outsiders that if you grew up in South Philadelphia during the '50s, you must have been on a first-name basis with all the home-grown neighborhood heroes: Mario Lanza, Eddie Fisher, Joey Bishop, Jack Klugman, James Darren, Fabian, David Brenner, Al Martino, and Frankie Avalon. Mario Lanza, the legendary operatic tenor and star of films like *The Student Prince* and *The Great Caruso,* was actually a close friend of my Uncle Joe (my Mom's brother), but I never met him.

When I was a kid, he was out in Hollywood, and then he died in 1959, when I was seventeen. Fisher, Bishop, Klugman, and Martino were older, established pros who had been out on the road for years, so our paths never crossed.

James Darren was the first guy from my generation to make it big. He played Moondoggie in the 1959 beach film *Gidget* and immediately followed that up with his first hit record, "Goodbye Cruel World." Everyone in South Philly heard about his triumphant drive down 11th Street in a shiny new convertible. Both he and Fabian lived only a few blocks away from me, but I never got to know either of them until after my own career was in full swing.

The lone exception to all these missed relationships was Frankie Avalon. We both shared similar beginnings as performers. I had my early moment in the sun on *The Paul Whiteman TV Teen Club*, and Frank's break came around the same time when he played "Tenderly" on trumpet on *The Jackie Gleason Show*. With both of us working the same local circuit as preteens, we got to know each other quite well. We were mostly performing at veterans hospitals, USO shows, and other small gigs, but on occasion, Frank would ask me to join him at The Frat, an underage club at 17th and Jackson.

Somewhere around 1955 or 1956, I joined a band called the Skylarks, in which I sang and played drums. Like most of the freelance work I was doing with other musicians in my early teens, we just played the popular music of the day. It was nothing too ambitious. We were all content to be gigging and having girls check us out when we were on stage.

One of my first TV appearances on the 1954 March of Dimes Telethon.

But there was one musician I worked with in a band called the Emanons (no-name spelled backwards) who was definitely hungering for more challenging material than the songs in our repertoire. He was a neighborhood guitarist named Patrick Azzara who was playing circles around everyone else. The Emanons' peak moment happened on TV when we played *Ted Mack's Amateur Hour,* but then—after less than a year—we all went our separate ways. Patrick Azzara went on to become Pat Martino, one of the all-time greats of jazz guitar.

In the summer of 1957, the drumming half of my budding career received a huge boost at the expense of one of my dad's fingers. He lost part of his middle finger in a work-related accident while operating some machinery. He could have done a lot of good things with the $3,000 settlement he received from his employer. He could have paid off some bills, taken a long overdue vacation with my mom, redecorated the house,

The Skylarks. I'm on the bottom row, second from the right.

The Emanons on the set of the "Ted Mack's Original Amateur Hour." I'm on the far right standing next to Ted, and second from the left is Pat (Azzara) Martino.

bought a new car . . . but no, not my dad. His first move was to buy me a $525, state-of-the-art, black oyster-pearl Ludwig drum set from 8th Street Music. This set wasn't relegated to the basement like my red Revere drums. It occupied a place of honor in our living room. (And why not? It probably cost more than the combined value of all the other furniture.)

My new drums couldn't have arrived at a more perfect time because I was starting to get gigs as a drummer. One of them came from Frankie Avalon, and would prove to be a turning point for me. Cheech—that was my nickname for him—was in a band called Rocco and the Saints. One night, they were booked as the opening act at a very popular club in Somers

The receipt from 8th Street Music for my black Ludwig drum set.

Point, New Jersey, called Bayshores. Chippie Peters, the band's drummer, was ill so Cheech asked me to fill in, sing a few tunes and do my usual imitations and comedy. The headliner that night was a prominent local act named Billy Duke and the Dukes, whose bass player was known as Frankie Day. (His real name was Francesco Cocchi.) Frankie must have liked what he saw and heard because he approached me after our set and said he'd like to manage me. I had no idea what that even meant so I just said, "Talk to my dad." I started the evening as a young kid going nowhere. An hour later after a handshake sealed the deal, I was an artist with a new direction and a manager. It was the summer of 1957.

36

Bayshores in Somers Point, New Jersey.

Frankie Day had no managerial experience; I had no recording experience. We were a perfect match. He was in his early 30s, but in spite of his relative youth, he acted with a great deal of urgency and purpose. Frankie's goal wasn't to get me steady work on the Philly and South Jersey club circuit; he went for the whole enchilada, right from the beginning. My dad was still dragging me around to play at any club in the area that had a house band. Frankie encouraged him to maintain that course, but within months, he'd also landed me auditions at major labels in New York, including RCA, Capitol, and Columbia. It was to no avail; there were no takers.

I gotta hand it to Frankie, though; he was far from being out of ideas or feeling defeated. He was just getting started. In 1958, he found a small label out of the Baltimore-Washington D.C. area called Veko that agreed to record me. The only red flag was we had to pick up the tab for the session, but it seemed like an acceptable risk. I cut three songs in one day: "Dream Age," "Fatty, Fatty," and "A Winner Can Lose." "Dream Age" was the first of the three, and on the master, I was out of tune and cursing under my breath. The other two songs didn't sound like they had much potential, either. It didn't matter; the two guys who ran Veko absconded with the tapes, and we never saw them again.

We did come out of the session with an acetate disc, but in all honesty, I wish they'd stolen that too. It led to one of the more embarrassing moments in my career. With a copy of "Fatty Fatty" in hand, Frankie landed me a radio interview on WAMO, a black radio station out of Pittsburgh. Sir Walter Raleigh and Porky Chedwick, two of the station's DJs, asked me if I wanted to participate in a record hop that night. The Crests, who were red hot, thanks to the overwhelming success of their signature track "Sixteen Candles," were the main attraction. A mostly African American crowd had turned out to see *them*—not this skinny, sixteen-year-old twerp lip-synching "Fatty Fatty Boom-Bolatty" to a crappy sounding disc. I felt like a total white-bread honky.

Maybe Frankie and my dad were pissed off and frustrated by the Veko affair, but other than making an ass of myself at the record hop, I wasn't that upset. In my mind, I had it all: natural talent, stage presence, boundless ambition and confidence, looks, and most importantly, I still had that absolutely *killer* pompadour. I was only missing one minor detail: an actual record contract.

🎼 VERSE 2

All too often, the answers we're looking for usually end up being right in front of our noses. It took Frankie Day a year to realize that he'd been looking in all the wrong places for that elusive record deal. The time and effort he spent going north to New York City and then south to Washington and Baltimore could have been better spent staying put. Just a few blocks from Philadelphia's City Hall was a small, independent label that was on the verge of becoming a major player in the teenage music market. It was named Cameo Records.

Cameo was started in 1956 by songwriters Bernie Lowe and Kal Mann in the basement of Bernie's West Oak Lane home. I had met Bernie back in 1952 when he was the keyboardist for *Paul Whiteman's TV Teen Club*. He and Kal had gotten off to a flying start penning "Teddy Bear" for Elvis Presley, and then landing a No. 1 record titled "Butterfly" with Cameo's first artist, singer-guitarist Charlie Gracie.

They added a subsidiary label called Parkway in 1958, and shortly after, moved into new downtown Philadelphia headquarters on the ninth floor of 1405 Locust Street. Hoping to find a diamond in the rough, they began holding auditions every Saturday from 9:00 a.m. until noon, during which they would tape up-and-coming local teenage singers and groups. The audition Frankie arranged for me was not what I expected. I thought Bernie would ask me to sing a song from my repertoire. Instead, he teamed me with another kid and asked us to sing a tune that I'd never heard before called "Buddies." I never saw the other kid again, but Bernie must have liked what I was doing because he signed me in January of '59. I was only sixteen years old.

Cameo got right down to business, cutting three songs with me in their primitive, monaural studio. My first experience recording for a big label might have overwhelmed me, but the three songs we cut—"Please Don't Be Mad," "All I Want Is You," and a tune penned by Paul Anka—weren't particularly exciting. "All I Want Is You," for instance, was basically the same song as "Stairway to the Stars," with a different melody. The intro, chords, and song structure were identical to the tired, old hit that Glenn Miller had made famous more than a decade-and-a-half before. All three records did nothing.

Years later "Please Don't Be Mad" became a cult hit. Sometimes I toy with the idea of combining that song and

I must have sung a bad note. Dave Appell is making a weird face in Cameo's studio.

the three Veko flops into a four-song medley that I could play live. I even have the perfect title: *The Who Gives A Shit Medley.*

My first recording session at Cameo wasn't a total waste though. The process showed me how things worked within the label. Although their roles changed somewhat in later years, Bernie usually wrote the music, Kal handled the lyrics, and Dave Appell, Cameo's Jack-of-all-trades, was the arranger, engineer, producer, and guitarist. All three of them were always on hand whenever I recorded, but it was Bernie who coached me as a singer, helping me with the pronunciation of my vowels and teaching me microphone technique. Cameo's house band came from a pool of local Philadelphia musicians that they had on call, and they also used members of Dave Appell's own band, the Applejacks. Having gained some knowledge and

41

understanding of the inner workings of the company's production line was probably a good thing, but it wasn't going to get me a hit. For the first time, I had some doubts. I didn't know what to think. For all I knew, Cameo was considering dropping me after I'd struck out three straight times. A few blocks away at "Idolmaker" Bob Marcucci's Chancellor Records, Frankie Avalon already had a huge smash with "Venus," and Fabian had scored with "Turn Me Loose."

Maybe it just wasn't in the cards for me. I made up my mind that regardless of what might happen, I'd be OK. A recording career would have been nice, but being a drummer and playing gigs for the rest of my life wasn't the worst thing in the world.

Surprisingly, those first three duds I cut for Cameo didn't faze Bernie and Kal in the least. They just went back to the drawing board. It didn't take them long to come up with the song that would kick-start my career. When "Kissin' Time" hit the airwaves in June of 1959, it triggered a seismic event that rippled through the company.

I sang the hell out of that tune, but the record's success wasn't all because of me. The track had a lot going for it: an irresistible hook in its ba-da-boom kick drum figure, the roster of city names in the lyric that personalized the song to a lot of fans in a lot of different markets, and then there was that flamethrower of a solo from future *Saturday Night Live* saxophonist Georgie Young.

My producer Dave Appell knew Georgie from their days of playing the Wildwood club circuit. Georgie and his band, the Rockin' Bocs, were a fixture at the Rainbow. Dave wanted a

The Rainbow in Wildwood, New Jersey with Georgie Young and the Rockin' Bocs name on the marquee.

harder driving rhythm section than the Applejacks for "Kissin' Time" so he recruited the Rockin' Bocs for the session. Then he sat back and watched them live up to their name. The wrecking ball of a beat they pumped out warped the studio's walls and loosened the nails and screws in the floorboards.

In addition, Cameo had a secret weapon in its corner that became the most important factor in breaking not only "Kissin' Time," but my career as well. Part of the key to Cameo's success was that it was located in Philadelphia, a few miles away from the No. 1 marketing tool in popular music at the time: Dick Clark's *American Bandstand*. Like *Paul Whiteman's TV Teen Club*, the show was broadcast weekday afternoons on ABC from local affiliate WFIL's 46th and Market Street studio.

43

With a national audience of almost twenty million viewers, it's easy to understand why Dick was considered to be the fast track to a hit record.

American Bandstand was the successor to Whiteman's show, on which Dick had worked as the announcer, and where he'd met Bernie Lowe. A mutually beneficial relationship between *Bandstand* and Cameo soon developed. Bernie and Kal would supply the show with a steady stream of acts and would bail out Dick with someone from their lineup whenever an artist from another label cancelled on him at the last moment. In return, Dick would expose Cameo's recordings to his national audience. He had a nose like a bloodhound when it came to sniffing out a hit, and luckily for me, he caught a strong scent of "Kissin' Time" and gave it his blessing. The song was released in mid-June. From the first moment he played the record on his show, the station's switchboard lit up. Philly was all in. Detroit, Boston, New York, Pittsburgh, and other cities followed suit. Within three weeks, it was the No. 11 record in the country.

I learned the news while I was playing ball in front of my grandmother's house in Wildwood. A neighbor came running over screaming, "Quick, turn on the radio. They're playing Bobby's record!" Then people started showing up on my steps back home in South Philly asking for autographs or wanting me to pose with them for pictures. If any of my friends were jealous, I didn't know it. Everyone seemed happy for me and extremely proud that someone from the neighborhood had made it. A few weeks later on August 4th, 1959, I was on *American Bandstand,* lip-synching "Kissin' Time" in front of what seemed like half the world. (I'd actually appeared on the show once before, giving a short interview after the release of "Please Don't Be Mad," but the song was such a bomb, no one paid any attention.)

At seventeen, I was still a lousy student and hated going to school. Cameo became my refuge. After Bernie signed me, I started playing hookey by taking the subway up to Locust Street and hiding out in Cameo's bathroom. I'd read comic books for a while, eat my lunch from a brown paper bag my mom had packed for me (usually a chicken salad sandwich), and then wait for school to be over before I headed back home. But after "Kissin' Time," I didn't have to do that anymore. It wasn't the smartest thing in the world to do, but I quit high school in my junior year. Most likely, I'd have done it anyway, even if I'd been Bishop Neumann's valedictorian. I was about to hit the road.

The gigs started right away. Frankie Day wasn't about to waste the momentum created by a nationwide hit. The majority of the dates were record hops, radio interviews, and some live gigs with pick-up bands who learned my material. Frankie, doing triple duty as my manager, conductor, and sometime bassist, also found me a steady drummer named Ray Deeley. I quickly learned how important a move that was, because even if the pick-up bands stunk (which was more often than I'd like to remember), at least our tempos remained consistent.

With a hit now under my belt, communication with Bernie Lowe became much more frequent. "OK, we got the first hit,"

Getting up close with my fans at an early concert.

he told me, "but the second and third ones will be much harder to achieve. We're working on some stuff for you." In a fatherly tone, he also advised me, "Let me and Frankie deal with the business. We'll be the pricks. You just play the role of the nice guy and worry about the music." I had that part covered. My family and the Old World Italian values I was raised on kept me grounded. I wasn't about to put on any airs. My father would see to that, and so would Frankie, who told me, "You're going to have to meet and deal with the same people on the way down as you did on the way up."

True to his word, Bernie soon had a new song for me that he and Kal had just written. It was the same deal as on

"Kissin' Time": Bernie wrote the music, Kal the lyrics, and Dave Appell arranged, produced, and played guitar. Except this time, it was a much larger production. We recorded it at Bell Sound in New York City with a cast of veteran studio musicians that included ace R&B drummer Panama Francis and eight background singers known as the Ray Charles singers. (Not *those* Ray Charles singers—these were the voices heard on *The Perry Como Show*). "We Got Love" was an infectious shuffle that cemented one of the key elements of my signature sound. You know those "Yeah, Yeah, Yeahs" you hear me singing in the choruses, the ones that answer the "We Got Love" exhortations of the background singers? It wouldn't be the last time fans of my records would hear that call-and-response technique.

The recording session was a textbook example of paralysis by analysis. It should have taken one day; somehow it took three. Bernie kept saying to Dave, "I can't hear the bass; where's the bass?" and we'd have to record it all over again. Come mixdown time, Dave and Bernie selected the second take from day one. Go figure.

"I can't hear the bass" was an all-too-familiar, annoying, almost Abbott and Costello type of refrain between Dave and Bernie. It usually went something like this:

DAVE (calling from a New York recording studio): Hey, Bernie, I just got finished cutting Bobby's new song. I think we got another hit!

BERNIE: Great. Play it for me over the phone.

DAVE: Bernie, it'll sound like crap through the phone. It'll be all tinny and you won't hear any bass.

BERNIE: I'm aware of that. Don't worry, just play it. I can visualize what it'll sound like when it's played on a good set of speakers. I just want to get the general feel and concept of the song.

DAVE (turning on the tape deck and holding the phone up to the speakers): Alright then, here goes . . . . .

BERNIE (listening to the playback through the phone): Sounds like shit. There's no bottom. Turn up the bass!

Bass or no bass, the two of them must have picked the right take because "We Got Love" bested the charted success of "Kissin' Time," reaching No. 6 on the *Billboard* pop charts. The album version became my first million seller. Two Top 40 hits to my name was enough to attract Dick Clark's attention when he put together his Fall of 1959 *Caravan of Stars* tour. With my head spinning around from my newfound success, I boarded one of the two buses that transported almost five dozen people on a forty-nine day tour of Canada, the East Coast, the Midwest, Texas, and a Hollywood Bowl performance in California.

Since I only had two records out, I was one of the lower tier acts on the tour's totem pole. Paul Anka was the headliner in a cast that included Duane Eddy, the Coasters, LaVern Baker, Freddy Cannon, Annette Funicello, and Jimmy Clanton, backed by Lloyd "Mr. Personality" Price's seventeen-piece big band.

This was the first of three Dick Clark *Caravans* that I performed in over the next few years, and I have to tell you, being a member of this traveling circus was an eye-opening experience. I'd never come across anything like the unusual antics and personal quirks of some of the more colorful characters in our traveling party.

There was LaVern Baker, who always wrapped herself up in a shower curtain so no one would touch her when she was sleeping on the bus. (LaVern's waking hours were usually spent accusing everyone of cheating in the blackjack games that routinely took place during the long road trips.) We had Bo Diddley on some of the shows, who repeatedly asked me to lend him one hundred dollars. I didn't take him seriously, although I couldn't say the same for Jerome Green. He was this brawny, tall guy in Bo's band who did nothing except dance around and play maracas. Throughout the tour, he kept coming up to me saying, "Bobby Rydell, lend me five hundred dollars." Unlike Bo, I wasn't sure if he really meant it or not. Either way, he terrified me. I meekly told him I was just a kid who didn't carry around that kind of money, and then clumsily tried to explain that whatever I made on the road was mailed back to my parents.

Jerome finally backed off, but was quickly replaced by another member of the cast who put my stomach in knots—for a much different reason. Cornelius Gunther was one of the singers in the Coasters. In today's politically correct climate, I guess it would be appropriate to describe him as "flamboyantly effeminate." In the less socially enlightened

My first Dick Clark Caravan of Stars tour.

atmosphere of the early '60s, the tendency was to call him a flaming queen or worse.

Regardless of the label, I'd had no experiences up to that point with anyone of the gay persuasion, so I was thrown into a panic when Cornelius approached me on the bus, batted his eyelashes and said, "Bobby Rydell, I had a dream about you last night." I did my best to disappear into the upholstery of my bus seat, but there was nowhere to hide. (And now that I think about it, why did all these guys keep referring to me as "Bobby Rydell" instead of just Bob or Bobby?)

For a young kid like me, the *Caravan of Stars* tour was a great place to learn the ropes of life on the road. Dick Clark was consumed by his many business ventures and was rarely around, so I was on my own without a chaperone. One night, Charlie Carpenter, the *Caravan's* tour manager, told us the bus was pulling out the next morning at 8:30 a.m. and if we weren't down in the lobby, they'd leave without us. My room-mate on the tour was Freddy Cannon of "Palisades Park" and "Tallahassee Lassie" fame. I overslept and found everyone was gone, including Freddy. The lone exception was Paul Anka, who had chosen to fly to the next city instead of take the bus. Thankfully, he took me along with him. (In those days, not every plane was overbooked weeks in advance like today.)

I was completely pissed off at Freddy, and backstage at the gig, I asked him why he hadn't woken me up before he'd gone down to the bus that morning. "You looked so nice sleeping there I didn't want to bother you," he answered as if it were the most logical explanation in the world. His response was so off-the-wall and stupid, it left me speechless. Nevertheless, I was the one who screwed up and overslept, so I just backed off. I'd learned a valuable lesson: The days of Mommy waking me up for school were over. I was a professional entertainer and I needed to start taking care of things myself.

The *Caravan of Stars* wasn't the kind of tour that set you up financially for the rest of the year. I was only making $500 a week for five or six weeks, but what I wasn't earning in cash, I was earning in experience. Dick Clark saw that I could now do more than just lip-synch, and we developed a stronger bond. I also got my name out there to a lot of new audiences, and returned home a seasoned performer, especially after playing large, intimidating venues like the Hollywood Bowl.

Best of all, I'd managed to avoid turning over my weekly earnings to Bo Diddley and his maraca player.

⊕　⊕　⊕

When the tour ended, I had no time to relax and unwind. My bookings and PR opportunities were up substantially and, while I didn't quite match Freddy Cannon's record one hundred and ten appearances on *American Bandstand,* I wasn't far behind. No one made money from appearing on the show anyway. It was all about PR. I became good friends with many of *Bandstand's* dancers, in part because it was just my nature as a kid off the streets, but also because you had to schmooze them. If they didn't like you, your records got no reaction,

Dick Clark plugging my latest record on the air.

especially when Dick did his "Rate-A-Record" segment of the show and asked the kids to vote for their favorite 45s.

My efforts didn't always work in my favor—at least not with *American Bandstand's* production staff. On one of the shows, my catering to the kids backfired on me. Whenever a guest recording artist appeared on *Bandstand*, the cast's dancers would temporarily take seats in the audience section of the studio. In the middle of one of my early lip-synch performances on the show, I went off my stage marker and walked into the audience to get closer to them. The director was furious and let me know in no uncertain terms that I was never to do that again.

In early 1960, Dave Appell accompanied me when I went up to New York to appear on Dick Clark's *Saturday Night Beech-Nut Show*. He started playing a song on his guitar and told me, "When we get back home, this'll be your next record." A week later I was in a Philly studio on 12th Street called Rec-O-Art. (Eight years later, it would become Sigma Sound Studios, the world-famous home of Gamble, Huff, and Bell's "Sound of Philadelphia" hits of the 1970s.) Emil Korsen, Rec-O-Art's owner, was a first-rate engineer, so sound-wise, I expected the track to be a significant jump over Cameo's rinky-dink, broom closet-of-a-studio. What I didn't expect was to wind up with a No. 2 pop hit, a million-seller, and my first gold single.

"Wild One" catapulted my career into a completely different orbit. I knew everything was going to change when I stopped by Cameo's office and saw the tallies from some of the distributors across the country: New York—100,000, Detroit—70,000, Boston—40,000, Chicago—65,000, Los Angeles—60,000. And then there were not just gigs, but offers for TV shows, magazine covers, overseas tours . . . it was hard to take it all in. So what was so special about this record that it created such a commotion?

For starters, Dave Appell got involved in the songwriting this time around and it showed. Dave had a great feel for the pop music of the times and he knew what pushed people's buttons. "Wild One" was a hook-fest of infectious rhythms and melodic twists that allowed me to dig in and show off my vocal chops—particularly my upper register. Joining me was a chorus of three black, female gospel singers (Willa Ward Moultrie, Vivian Jackson, and Mary Wiley) who Dave used to great effect to solidify my sound's identifiable style. Remember the "Yeah, Yeahs" on "We Got Love?" Well now, we added "Whoa, Whoas." How could I miss with award-winning lyrics like that?

The Applejacks were back as studio musicians, augmented by drum royalty. Gary Chester—a nice Italian boy whose real name was Cesario Gurciullo (and make sure you roll the R's)—was a bona fide hit-maker with a resume of chart-toppers a mile long. The rhythmic stability and drive of the track stood out from most of what was riding the airwaves at the time.

With all that happening, it's easy to overlook the overall sound of the record, but "Wild One" had a magical ambience that has to be attributed one hundred percent to Emil Korsen and one of his sonic signatures. Emil placed a speaker and a microphone in the bathroom and fed the sound back to the mixing board. Whatever I sang on the floor came through the speaker and then was picked up—along with the bathroom's ceramic tiled ambience—by the mic. If you listen carefully, you can probably hear a toilet flush in the background. Phil Spector's "Wall of Sound" had nothing on Emil.

Several months later, the Cameo brain trust tried to recreate the same hit-making formula we used on "Wild One." Same studio, same background singers with the "Whoa Whoas," same songwriting team, same Applejacks back-up band, but with one minor exception: no Gary Chester. The result was "Swingin' School," which topped out at No. 5 on the *Billboard* charts. (I guess Gary's drumming accounts for "Wild One's" additional three spots on the Top 10 chart.)

I recorded two versions of "Swingin' School": the hit version and an additional one for Dick Clark's film *Because They're Young*. That may seem like an insignificant detail, but the timing was perfect. Because the song was prominently featured in the film, it gave me continued national visibility during a period in which I'd be overseas. I was heading to Australia.

In June of 1960, a promoter named Lee Gordon had hooked up with Frankie Day and booked me on a show that starred the Everly Brothers, the Crickets, the Champs, Santo and Johnny, the Diamonds, a country-rockabilly singer named Billy "Crash" Craddock, and Motown's Marv Johnson. My father and Frankie accompanied me on the trip. Dad came along for moral support, and Frankie, as usual, handled the business and conducted. Lee Gordon shelled out big bucks for first-class Pan Am tickets for all of us.

When we landed in Sydney and saw thousands of kids at the airport to welcome us, Phil and Don Everly and I looked at each other and smiled, thinking we were in for one hell of a tour. Those smiles lasted about ten seconds; all the kids ran right past us and mobbed Billy Craddock. Who the hell was this guy? We had no idea. Then we learned that his record "Boom, Boom Baby" was the No. 1 hit in Australia that week.

Regardless, the rest of the tour couldn't have been better. Our Australian fans turned out in droves. A lot of my personal success down under was due to a gentleman named Brian Henderson, who was Australia's Dick Clark. He had a TV show similar to *American Bandstand* on which he'd heavily promoted my records, while simultaneously painting an image of me as "the guy next door." In fact, thanks to Brian, I cut an alternate version of "Kissin' Time," substituting Australian cities for the American ones in the original lyric. It was a huge hit throughout the tour. I can't say the attention I received from city to city was comparable to Beatlemania, but when the police have to form a wedge to get you to and from the stage, it's not something you easily forget.

That 1960 show was the first date of a more than half-century love affair between the Australian people and me. Over the last five decades, I've toured there twenty-two different times.

Playing drums on my first Australian tour.

⊕   ⊕   ⊕

What was the relationship between an Italian love song, a tune that was originally a 1953 mambo, and an old standard written by Harold Arlen and Johnny Mercer? This wasn't a set of hints for a question on a TV game show. It was the trio of songs I faced when I walked into New York's RCA studios in the spring of 1960, a few weeks before I took off for Australia. Cameo had slated all three for an upcoming album. The album was never released, but eventually, Cameo put them out as singles and staggered their release dates.

The first of them was "Volare," whose success surprised the hell out of me. "Wild One" sounded like a hit even before it was mixed, but "Volare?" Naaah!! I thought we were just cutting it because they needed a follow-up to "Swingin' School" or a filler song for the album. The last thing in the world I expected was for it to chart at No. 4 and become a million-seller and my career-long theme song. To this day, when you see me live, that's my walk-on and walk-off song at the beginning and end of my shows.

When "Volare" first hit the airwaves in 1958, it became an international smash for its composer and singer, Domenico Modugno. A few years later, Dean Martin also had a hit with it. In a press release, Cameo said that the selection of the song was my mother's idea, but that was just a public relations move. Dave Appell, who arranged and co-produced my version, must have figured "how could he lose with a song that had that kind of track record?" (Speaking of records, "Volare" was the first of my recordings to come out with Cameo's fancy new red and black label, which replaced the original all-orange design on 45s like "Kissin' Time" and "Wild One.")

The second tune of the three, "Sway," was a riskier proposition than "Volare" because it was a Latin tune. It was a new direction for me. I'd never sung anything like that before. Again, Dave selected and arranged it, but he played it safe by relying once again on a security blanket of background vocal "Yeah, Yeahs" and "Whoa, Whoas." Nevertheless, the song that was added just to fill up tracks on the album turned out to be a shrewd choice; it proved I was much more than just a rock and roll singer.

The third tune of the group, "That Old Black Magic," was the least imaginative of the three. By picking such a well-worn standard, I felt that Dave was taking the easy way out, but I changed my mind after I heard the arrangement. The last thing I'd have expected was for him to transform the tune into a saxophone-honking rocker with a slick, Hollywood Bowl string and vocal intro. ("Good Time Baby, " which was cut in January of '61 back at Rec-O-Art in Philadelphia, was built around an almost identical unison sax line and groove.)

Neither "Sway" nor "That Old Black Magic" cracked the Top 10, but the former has endured as a favorite of my live shows, especially in The Land Down Under. A few years ago when I told an Australian audience that "Sway" was one of the first tunes Michael Bublé ever recorded, someone shouted out, "You do it better than him, mate!" Whether it's true or not, I appreciated the sentiment.

TEEN IDOL ON THE ROCKS

☥   ☥   ☥

By 1961, I realized that I'd been singing incorrectly for years. I began to lose my chops. I should have taken up Artie Singer on his suggestion to come back for singing lessons after my teenage voice changed. A few people suggested I see a New York City vocal coach named Marty Lawrence. When I entered his studio for the first time, I could barely talk. An hour later, everything was wide open. Marty put me back on track, getting me to sing from the diaphragm instead of just using my throat. I used to call him the Professor because I was so impressed and grateful for how much he helped me.

It was crucial that I regained my voice at this specific time. The gig of my life was coming up: I was scheduled to play the Copacabana in New York for a ten-day run, and at the age of nineteen, I was going to be the youngest headliner ever to perform in that landmark club's history.

With a gig that important, there was no way Frankie Day was going to let me walk on that stage with my usual program, which was, "just go out there and sing your hits." The basic musical arrangements I'd been using for my live shows wouldn't cut it at a venue like the Copa, so he brought in an arranger named Joe Zito to rewrite my book and conduct. Frankie, who'd done an admirable job handling the conducting chores during the early stages of my career, was smart enough to know that he was out of his league when it came to directing a musical ensemble the level of the Copa's in-house orchestra.

Also, most significantly, he overhauled the show's basic concept. I have no idea where Frankie learned about or found them, but he hired Lou Spencer and Noel Sherman to produce and re-stage my entire act. Lou was originally one-third of a highly regarded tap dance trio called the Dunhills. They'd come to prominence after appearing in a Betty Grabel film titled *Call Me Mister* in 1951, and then had a stellar decade-and-a-half run making the rounds of TV variety shows like *The Ed Sullivan Show, The Texaco Star Theater,* and *The Frank Sinatra Show.* When Lou's career as a performer was over, he partnered up with lyricist and stage producer Noel Sherman, and they became an in-demand duo that coached nightclub acts like Nat King Cole and others. It was heady stuff for a teenaged kid like me to even think about working with battle-tested pros like these two guys.

We rehearsed in a New York studio for several weeks. Noel wrote all my scripted banter and handpicked the songs, jokes, and schticks that I'd perform throughout the show. Lou took care of how it all looked, agonizing over every detail, like where I stood, how I moved, my facial expressions, timing, and my overall stage presence. They worked me hard and didn't pull any punches when it came to analyzing and critiquing what I was doing. A lot of coaches might have taken it easy on me because of my age, but not these guys, and not Lou in particular.

They used my appearance at the Three Rivers Inn in Syracuse, New York as a dress rehearsal for the Copa. I came off the stage thinking I'd just put on a helluva show; Lou had other ideas. Walking into my dressing room afterwards, he grabbed a roll

Going over my dance steps with Lou Spencer.

of toilet paper and tore off two or three individual sheets. Holding them up in front of my face, he said, "This is what you did right." Then he showed me the entire roll and added, "This is what you did wrong." What a ball-breaker he was.

Yet, nobody panicked, not me or anyone else. There were no rewrites, no words of consolation, or last-minute attempts to build up my confidence. I wasn't going to curl up in a fetal position. I knew what I was doing and I believed in myself. So did my team. What's that old show biz saying? "Bad rehearsal, great performance?" That's exactly what happened.

When I hit the stage at the Copa the first night, the club was packed so tightly the Copa Girls had no room to dance their opening production number. Thanks to Lou and Noel, my show had it all: sensitive ballads like "Don't Be Afraid to Fall in Love," a medley from the Broadway show *Gigi*, black jump blues tunes like "Open the Door Richard" and Louis Jordan's "Caldonia," plus Al Jolson's "Mammy," a comedic skit built around a song Noel wrote called "They Don't Write Them Like That Anymore" that spoofed novelty songs of the past, and, of course, my Cameo hits.

The reviews were staggeringly good, with headlines like, "A Powder Keg of Talent," "Rydell A Smash In Copa Debut," and "Bobby Rydell Captures Copa." The critics also singled out Noel and Lou's expert staging, and even Frankie Day earned praise from *Variety* for "steering me in the right direction." The most telling evidence of my potential as more than a flash-in-the-pan pop star was lost on me amidst all the excitement: I'd just wowed an audience made up of mostly adults. I was

Reviews from my first gig at the Copacabana.

still a hit, even without my usual audience of screaming teenagers. Was this a one-time fluke, or could I really make it in traditional, adult venues? I got an immediate opportunity to test that theory. As soon as I completed the Copa shows, I jetted to Vegas to begin a four-week run at the Sahara with George Burns.

I may have just been the opening act, but this was a big deal. It was my Las Vegas debut and right out of the box, I'm working with a legend like George—and at the Sahara, no less. My first thought was to fly my parents out to see the first few nights. Thanks to the money I'd earned from five hit records, I'd helped my dad retire earlier in the year. He accompanied me on a lot of my road trips as my unofficial tour manager and driver. My mom, on the other hand, rarely came to shows that were outside of the immediate Philadelphia area, but she sure as hell was coming to this one. Seeing the look of pride on their faces when they read my name on the Sahara's marquee was a very special moment for me.

As for George, he took a liking to me right away, offering me advice and becoming protective in a fatherly sort of way. A few nights into the run he warned me—half in jest—"Don't let me catch you in the casino or I'll bop you in the head." I tried to thank him, but my good intentions boomeranged. On a night when we had two performances, I took George and Frankie Day out to an Italian restaurant in between the early and late shows. By the time we left, I radiated garlic from every pore of my body. My breath alone would have chased off a battalion of vampires.

George and I had a comedic bit based on an old song Sophie Tucker made famous called "Some of These Days." George sang his lines vaudeville style and I counterpunched, swinging mine like I was Cab Calloway working in front of a big band. That night, George wouldn't have cared if I sang it like Little Richard, Luciano Pavarotti, or Lena Horne. He was too pissed off at me for polluting his space every time we came near each other.

φ   φ   φ

Some months after my debut at the Copa, my dad, Frankie Day and I drove up to New York City to see singer-comedian

My garlic breath and George Burn's stinky cigar.

Joe E. Lewis, who was appearing at the club. In 1957, Frank Sinatra had portrayed him in the film *The Joker Is Wild,* and unbeknownst to me, he was in the house that night to see his old friend perform. Carmine, the maitre d', came up to me as I was checking my coat and asked if I wanted to sit with Frank. At first, I thought he meant Frankie Day, until I realized he was referring to Sinatra. I was so nervous and intimidated I declined the offer.

At the end of the show, Sinatra gets up and leaves, and I'm thinking to myself, "Idiot! You had your chance and you blew it." I was morose. I'd wasted the opportunity to meet one of my all-time heroes. With my tail between my legs, I went to the upstairs lounge to say goodbye to Jules Podell. Uncle Julie—as he asked me to call him—was the guy who ran the Copa. Just as we started to talk, who should come walking out of the kitchen door but Sinatra and a group of his friends. His entourage for the night included Joe DiMaggio, songwriters Sammy Cahn and Jimmy Van Heusen, and actor Richard Conti. I wasn't going to blow it a second time. I told Jules about what had happened downstairs before the show and would you believe it? He walks me right over to where Sinatra and his boys were seated. "Frank," he announced, "I want you to meet the kid."

I would have been more than happy with just a quick handshake, but Frank smiled at me and said, "How ya doin', Robert. Would you like to join us?" Then he asked me what I was drinking. I nursed a Coke for the next hour and took it all in. He really went out of his way to make me feel a part of his entourage, and then posed for a picture with me and signed a copy of my *Live At The Copa* album. I headlined the club three or four more times before it finally closed its doors in 1973. After Uncle Julie had died earlier that year, everyone knew its days were numbered. It was the end of a glorious era.

I never forgot Sinatra's gracious acceptance of me that night. He made me feel like I belonged on that club's hallowed stage. Over the years, I ran into Frank a few more times. A particularly memorable reunion occurred seven years later in front of twenty thousand people at the Philadelphia Spectrum. He was in town campaigning for Hubert Humphrey's presidential run, which happened to coincide with a previously booked concert date. Midway through the show, Frank told the audience, "I'd like to introduce you all to a friend of mine in the house tonight who's an old-fashioned saloon singer

Frank Sinatra, me, my dad, and Frankie Day at the Copa.

like me. My good friend . . ." and just at that moment, TV talk show host Mike Douglas started to stand up, thinking he was going to name him. Instead, Frank finished the sentence by naming *me*. "Where are you Bobby," he said as the spotlight searched for me among the mass of people seated in front of the stage. Once it found me, Frank blew me a kiss and I blew one back at him.

It was an embarrassing moment for Mike, who slumped dejectedly back into his seat. He was a friend of mine, and I felt bad for him. Still, it would have been impossible for me—or anyone else—not to feel elated to get the seal of approval from the Chairman of the Board in front of (what seemed like) half the population of Philadelphia.

A few years later I found out that a particular record of mine was the reason behind it all. Frank Sinatra, Jr. and I were doing a guest spot on Sid Mark's syndicated all-Sinatra radio show, when midway through our interview, Sid said, "Frank, you once said you thought Bobby was one of the best singers around." "I didn't say that," Frank Jr. said. "My father did. When he heard 'Sway,' he told me, 'Now here's a kid who can really sing.'" (Once again, thank you, Dave Appell, for picking—what seemed to me at the time to be—a risky song.)

That record changed a lot of things for me, not just in the greater volume of offers coming in, but also the variety of those offers. The concerts and nightclubs were predictable, but now Frankie Day was getting calls for me to appear on TV variety shows, made-for-TV pilots, movie proposals, and an avalanche of requests from teen and movie magazines like *16, Hit Parader, Teen Magazine, Motion Picture,* and *Photoplay.*

Frankie's job became increasingly demanding. He was smart enough to realize that just rolling the dice and fielding whatever concert offers came in wouldn't cut it. Instead, he was completely focused on building a lasting career for me—one that would showcase and exploit all the facets of my talents.

The magazines were the easiest part. As soon as he hired a New York publicity agent named Connie DeNave, everything snowballed. It seemed that every week, another magazine had a "Win a Date with Bobby" contest, or an article about what I liked in girls, what kind of girls I didn't like, or whether I was dating Annette Funicello, Shelley Fabares, or some other starlet.

General Artists Corporation (GAC) began handling my TV bookings, or should I say—in a good way—my TV "over-bookings." I had the good fortune to spend my peak years as a recording artist during the golden age of the TV variety show. Throughout the early '60s, I appeared on almost all of them—Ed Sullivan, Perry Como, Jack Benny, Jimmy Dean, George Burns, Joey Bishop, Milton Berle, Danny Thomas, Red Skelton—and most of them numerous times. The shows usually asked me to sing and almost always involved me in various production numbers and comedy skits. That added up to a lot of rehearsing. Thankfully, I was a quick study.

I got along with all of the TV hosts, but my favorites were Milton, Danny, and Red. I played Milton's show several times, and as preparation for one of them, I got to record a song he composed titled, "You Gotta Enjoy Joy." It was the show's theme song. We cut it in Los Angeles with a big band that featured jazz pianist Bob Florence, one of my all-time drum heroes, Louis Bellson, and bassist Carol Kaye, of the famed West Coast studio band, the Wrecking Crew. It was released as a single, but with its gimmicky title, there wasn't much of a chance that it would make any waves.

Danny Thomas invited me to appear on *Make Room for Daddy* in 1960. I played the role of a wise-ass kid. As an eighteen-year-old pop star, it wasn't that much of a stretch, as you can imagine. Danny also named me the teenage president of ALSAC (Aiding Leukemia-Stricken American

I had Jack Benny's signature pose down pat, don't you think?

Danny Thomas was a better pool player than me, but I had the better hair.

Children), his St. Jude's Hospital charity. I held the post for several years, and then Bobby Vinton took over.

Red Skelton and I were extremely close—almost like family. For a variety of reasons, my relationship with him was much more involved than with the other TV show hosts. I think I reminded him of his son, Richard, who had passed away from leukemia at the age of fifteen. I first played his show in 1960 and became a regular, appearing at least a dozen times over the next four to five years. Remember his famed role as Clem Kadiddlehopper? Horsing around on the set, I did such a good job of imitating him that Red and his producer Cecil Barker decided to create a character for me named Zeke Kadiddlehopper—Clem's younger cousin.

I always used to address him as "Mr. Skelton," even after he urged me to call him "Red." I wouldn't do it; it made me feel uncomfortable. It just seemed disrespectful. His response was to start calling me "Mr. Rydell," so we eventually agreed to use our first names. After one of my appearances, he invited me to his house in Palm Springs. Apparently it was a big deal, his wife told me, because he never invited anyone there. I spent the weekend and then he had his private plane fly me back to L.A. Before I left, we posed by his pool for a picture that was going to run in a local magazine. Red always had a big, colorful bird on his shoulder called a macaw. He told me to put my arm around his shoulder as we posed for the shot, and wouldn't you know it, the damn bird bit me! Red laughed so hard, he almost fell in the pool. *Now* I laugh about it too, but at the time, I didn't think it was so funny.

Another incident I also didn't find much humor in involved my grandmother. On a rare, free night in 1962, I went out on the town to see Sammy Davis, Jr. perform at the Latin Casino in Cherry Hill, New Jersey. We'd met the previous year at the Copa and really hit it off. Greeting me backstage following the show, he asked me, "Bobby, when are you gonna invite me over to your house for a good, home-cooked Italian meal?" Now you gotta understand, with Sammy being a card-carrying member of the Rat Pack, this became a sacred duty for me. I couldn't

At Red Skelton's home in Palm Springs with his family and his man-eating macaw.

have Frank Sinatra being pissed at me for not taking good care of his close friend. On the spot, I invited Sammy to come over on the first off-day he had during his run at the Latin.

My grandmother really went to town, cooking up a huge spread: escarole soup, pasta, sausage and meatballs, broccoli rabe—the whole deal. Sammy was thrilled and I was relieved when everything went off without a hitch. Regrettably, those reactions were short-lived. A few minutes after finishing off the main course, Sammy was convulsing with laughter, and I was wringing my hands and cringing in humiliation. Grandma Lena had come out of the kitchen with a huge plate of watermelon for dessert.

When I looked at her with an "I can't believe you just did that" stare, she defensively replied, "What? What? I thought that's what *they* liked." Bless her heart, she had a sense that she'd committed some type of faux pas, even if she wasn't exactly sure what it was.

✢   ✢   ✢

Frankie Day and Cameo's front office had spent my first three years at the label carefully building my career. For the most part, they did a masterful job. They really knew where to direct their marketing efforts, particularly in the U.S., targeting East Coast and Midwest urban centers like Boston, New York, Philly, Washington, D.C., Miami, Chicago, Pittsburgh, Cleveland, and Detroit. Los Angeles and Las Vegas were also eventually integrated into the mix, but Frankie, Bernie and Kal were realistic about places like Nebraska, Wyoming, Utah, and the deep South. They knew that no matter how hard they worked, my ethnic Italian, teen idol appeal wasn't going to gain much traction there.

In my mind—other than having *American Bandstand* as my neighborhood promotional outlet—the most valuable player in my career development may have been my fan club network.

It was an absolutely ingenious pre-Internet, get-the-word-out, cross-country grid of devoted fans who lovingly documented my every move. There were a lot of heroes involved, but none deserved kudos more than Frankie Day and a Philadelphia-area teenager named Linda Ferrino. I first met Linda at one of my Steel Pier shows in Atlantic City. Actually, my mom—ever the social facilitator—met Linda and her mother at one of the shows and introduced us. Linda knew everything about me. To this day, I have no idea how she was privy to some of the things in my life that she knew about.

Frankie was quick to recognize a winning hand when he saw one. After he anointed Linda the national president of my fan club, the two of them worked for months on finding like-minded teenagers across the country to direct regional and local Bobby Rydell fan clubs. Communication between all the moving parts was via mass mailings of postcards that kept everyone abreast of all my career developments. The payoff for everyone was special perks and access to me when I toured near them. Further down the chain, the fans who paid a few dollars for their annual membership received newsletters, signed pictures, Bobby Rydell buttons, and other enticements.

I was touched by everyone's devotion back then and even more so today. A half-century down the road, Linda Ferrino (now Linda Hoffman) still runs my fan club. It's why I still have a career.

My fan club president, Linda Ferrino

Too bad they didn't have frequent flyer miles in 1961 because I was logging some serious distances. The long car rides of 1959 and '60 quickly became a thing of the past. I was flying out to the West Coast constantly and Frankie Day was also landing me overseas jobs. The increased visibility from my TV appearances and the word-of-mouth from my successes at the Copa and the Sahara resulted in gigs in Japan, Hong Kong, Australia, and Europe. I arrived in London off a horrific thirty-four hour flight from Sydney, Australia and taped a *Live From the London Palladium* TV show, then traveled on to concert dates in Sweden, the Tivoli in Copenhagen, and both the Olympia and the Palais des Sports in Paris for the Festival du Rock.

Deplaning in Los Angeles with Frankie Day.

Singing on the "Live from the London Palladium" TV show.

A separate trip to the San Remo Festival on the Italian Riviera came as a welcome surprise when I found out I'd be performing with Frankie Avalon and Gene Pitney. Cheech and I had lost touch since he moved to the West Coast to do his series of beach movies. It was good to be with him again. Each of us had to perform two songs in Italian. My two were "Un Bacio Piccolisimo"("One Tiny Kiss") and "Ilverno Cose Fai." ("I have no friggin' idea what this means.") While in Italy, I got to meet Domenico Modugno, who invited me to visit him at his villa in Rome. Singing "Volare" with him in his home was more than anyone had a right to ask for. I must have done something good in a previous life.

So by now you're probably wondering, "Here's this young kid jetting all over the world where beautiful, teenaged girls are

Singing "Volare" with Domenico Modugno at his villa in Rome.

dancing to his records and screaming and squealing in their seats at his concerts. He must have had one wild time." Well, not as much as you may think. From 1960 through 1964, I was on the road eight to ten months a year, and there was very little time for me to do much other than perform, do PR, travel to the next town, and grab a little bit of rest when I could. I was very young and inexperienced, but I'm not complaining; I eventually did have my moments.

For decades, I've done a routine in my act during which I strut around the stage and boast about having had my first sexual encounter under the boardwalk in Wildwood when I was thirteen. The set-up and punchline? "I was scared y'know because . . . I was all alone." (The rim shot on the drums makes it much better, I swear to you!)

In real life, my very first sexual encounter actually occurred four thousand miles west of Wildwood in the Hollywood Roosevelt Hotel when I was seventeen. Bernie, Kal, Dave, and Frankie Day had come out to the West Coast with me for a TV appearance. They were hanging out in the living room of our suite while I was trying to take a nap in one of the bedrooms. I noticed the doorknob turning and all of a sudden, in walks a devastatingly hot-looking woman. Those guys had decided to put an end to my virginity and hired me a hooker. I was nervous, but she was sweet and very gentle.

My second and third experiences happened a few years later and weren't as innocent or as much fun. One was in a brothel in Cologne, Germany. The girl was a big, demanding woman who looked like a Nazi stormtrooper. Definitely not my thing.

The other took place in Paris the night I played the Olympia. After the show, Frankie and I decided to get two hookers. The girls seemed friendly enough, but as soon as we got back to our hotel room, they rushed us through everything and then demanded an exorbitant fee. Five minutes later, they were gone. Frankie and I looked at each other and said—almost in unison—"Did we just get fucked, or did we just get fucked?" If anything could be credited for driving me into the arms of Camille and getting more serious about our relationship, those two nights would definitely be high on the list.

But as usual, the demands of my career pushed any self-assessment of my life and values into the background. Bookings and requests for interviews continued to pour in. I spent six weeks in 1962 on my third (and last) Dick Clark *Caravan* co-headlining with Frankie Avalon on a murderous schedule that hit a new city every night. There was also an appearance at the Hollywood Bowl in the middle of that run—the second of three from 1961 through 1963. In the '61 show, I was on a bill with Jan and Dean, Chubby Checker and Freddy Cannon. I heard the '63 show set an attendance record with over five thousand tickets sold, but it was the 1962 Hollywood Bowl show that meant the most to me. The reason? The band that backed us up was the Nelson Riddle Orchestra. You can imagine what a thrill it was for me to meet and work with the cat who'd arranged "I've Got You Under My Skin," "In the Wee Small Hours of the Morning," "Nice 'N Easy," and so many other masterpieces from Frank Sinatra's catalog.

When I got home from the tour, all the highs I'd experienced with the *Caravan* and at the Hollywood Bowl soon faded under the weight of new challenges and responsibilities. For starters, I had a new drummer to break in. Ray Deeley had a wife and kid back home who'd been getting the short end of the stick for some time, and he had wearied of life on the road. Sight unseen and without hearing as much as a single note at an audition, I hired his replacement on reputation alone. Fellow South Philadelphian (actually Southwest Philly) Carl Mottola was the new hotshot drummer around town. He'd studied with the guy Sam D'Amico had suggested I study with (but never did)—New York City drum teacher Sam "Mr. Rhythm" Ulano.

Carl showed up on my doorstep one day with a full drum kit ready to hit the road. He was an impressive looking guy with a lean, powerful, six foot four inch frame and a chiseled face that looked like it belonged on top of a Roman statue. Best of all, he was a disciple of the same drum background I loved: Buddy Rich, Louie Bellson, Joe Morello, Ed Shaughnessy . . . I had a feeling we'd be traveling together for a long time.

At local nightclubs like South Philly's Palumbo's and Sciolla's at 5th and Pike, Carl and I developed and nurtured a new component of my show that quickly became a fan favorite. Two full drum kits were set up and Carl and I would tear it up in a good old-fashioned Gene Krupa versus Buddy Rich style drum duel. The vehicle for this knockdown, drag-out battle of paradiddles and ratamacues was the

Carl Mottola and me going at it in front of a packed house at Sciolla's.

old Duke Ellington big-band standard, "C Jam Blues." It really breathed some new life into my act and always elicited loud hoots and hollers from my audiences.

So with my revitalized stage show, a new book of charts, a hard-grooving new drummer, half-a-dozen hit records, and an increasingly impressive television resume, I could feel something big was on the horizon; I just hoped that whatever it turned out to be would live up to my growing expectations.

♪ CHORUS 2

Frankie Day and GAC had been burning up the phone lines for weeks. There was talk that I was being considered for a role in a film version of the 1960 hit Broadway musical, *Bye Bye Birdie*. Frankie had been working hard on diversifying my career ever since he saw how easily I handled the short skits on all my TV variety show appearances. In the early '60s, he'd landed me two TV pilots: The first one, *Swingin' Together*, paired me with Stephanie Powers in a show about a rock and roll band traveling around the country in a bus. In the second, I worked with William Bendix on a military comedy called *Rockabye the Infantry*. I played a G.I. on an Army base running a baby-sitting service to make some extra cash. Besides the lame titles, both of them had predictable, corny scriptwriting, and neither one amounted to much of anything. I hoped my third time in front of a camera would be the charm.

Frankie Day and me at the Surf Club in Wildwood

Bye Bye Birdie's storyline and principal character were loosely based on the hysteria that swept across America in 1957 when Elvis Presley was drafted into the Army. "Conrad Birdie"—the film's Elvis parody—was a bit of wordplay on the stage name of one "Harold Lloyd Jenkins," better known as Conway Twitty. One of Elvis' rock and roll rivals in the late '50s, Twitty eventually switched over to country music some years later.

If Conway Twitty could pull off such a dramatic career about-face, then so could I. I wasn't what anyone would refer to as a trained actor. I'd never taken any lessons or even appeared in so much as a high school play. Yet I was too young and cocky to consider those limitations or what the fallout would be if I fell flat on my face. The opportunity was so intriguing that I didn't allow any negative thoughts to enter my brain. In fact, there wasn't much time to think about it at all because before I knew it, a screen test had been scheduled at Columbia Pictures with the film's director, George Sidney.

I was auditioning for the role of Hugo Peabody, the nerdy, jealous boyfriend of Kim McAfee, a Conrad Birdie fan from Ohio who won a nationwide contest to give him his last kiss before he went off to the Army. I wasn't the only one after that part. Bobby Vinton—a very accomplished artist in his own right—was also in the running. But once I found out that my screen test partner was Ann-Margret, who was playing the role of Kim, I was determined to beat him out. There was no way I was going to blow an opportunity to work with a mega-talented, drop-dead knockout like her.

The screen test was mostly predictable and straightforward. I talked to the camera and told everyone about myself, read a few solo lines from the Broadway script, and then Ann and I read some lines together. But then the audition went off course from what I expected. George Sidney asked Ann and me to sing a song from the show titled "One Boy." In the Broadway production, Hugo didn't dance or sing, and he had very few lines. By considering Bobby Vinton and me, the movie director and producers clearly intended to capitalize on our singing abilities in the film version of the show.

Overall, I thought I had a very strong audition and had a good shot at landing the role. In the meantime, all I could do was return home and wait out the decision-making process.

George Sidney directing a rehearsal with Ann and me.

As you can guess, by this point in my career, that didn't mean sitting in my living room staring at the phone and hoping it would ring. "Home" meant getting back into the recording studio and hitting the road.

Of the three charted songs I recorded in 1962, only one reached the Top 10. "I've Got Bonnie" placed at No. 18, and "I'll Never Dance Again" came in at No. 14, but "The Cha-Cha-Cha" sneaked in at No. 10. Its impact overseas was much more significant than its chart position implied, particularly down in Australia. It hit so big there, I had to do a follow-up to my 1960 tour with the Everly Brothers. The

90

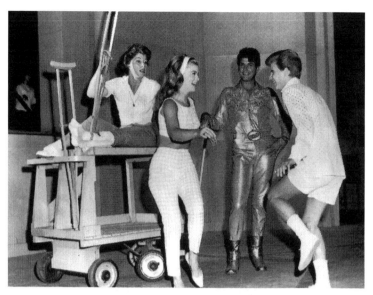

"Bye Bye Birdie" choreographer Onna White (with her leg in a cast and with crutches) teaches Ann and me a dance sequence while Conrad Birdie (Jesse Pearson) looks on.

highlight was a weeklong engagement at Club Chequers in Sydney, during which I broke the venue's all-time attendance record set by Shirley Bassey. Dennis Wong, the club's owner, was so thrilled that he invited me to his home for an authentic Chinese dinner. It was a great honor that, awkwardly, included a delicacy called "Eye of the Fish." Somehow, I got it down.

When I returned home, Frankie called with the good news that I'd landed the *Bye Bye Birdie* role. Filming began in late 1962 and lasted almost five months. I really enjoyed acting, but I quickly came to the conclusion that I like singing much better. I wasn't wild about all the hurry-up-and-wait, the 6:00

a.m. make-up calls, and the sitting in your trailer for five hours waiting for your turn in front of the camera. But other than those minor gripes, I had little to complain about. My Hugo character grew in the script, when George Sidney took advantage of the magic he saw between Ann and me and milked it as much as possible. The "One Boy" duet between us became a major feature as did the dance sequence on "A Lot of Livin' To Do." They added additional singing parts for me on "Rosie" and "We Love You Conrad," and you gotta' love the right cross I delivered to Conrad Birdie's chin. The toughest neighborhood bully back at Jenks schoolyard in South Philly would have given it his seal of approval. Overall, I couldn't have asked for a better role for a first shot at a feature film.

Sometimes I'd be off for a few weeks between my scenes. Fred Kohlmar, the film's producer, asked me to remain in L.A. during those down periods, and to avoid going to the beach so my skin tone and color would remain constant throughout the filming. When I was working, the on-set hang during principal photography made the job all the more enjoyable. Dick Van Dyke, Janet Leigh, Paul Lynde, and Maureen Stapleton were all marvelous people to be around and work with. There wasn't a single instance of ego-itis or diva behavior—at least, not during the filming period. The premiere was a different story.

I wasn't at the film's Hollywood debut, but heard that Janet Leigh angrily stormed out of the theater after she saw the sex-kitten treatment given to some of Ann's scenes. By today's standards, it was very tame "G" rating footage, but apparently Janet felt Ann's gyrating hips and torso got too much attention

Ann and me meeting Prince Philip at our Royal Audience.

and she felt slighted. I made the Philadelphia premiere and more importantly, the film's debut in London, where Ann and I had a command performance for the Royal Family and got to meet Prince Philip.

With the filming of the movie behind us, London afforded Ann and me our first opportunity to spend time together in a non-working environment. We had a light-hearted, flirty thing going on, but we both knew our futures lay elsewhere. My gut told me that my friendship with Ann would prove to be far more valuable and long-lasting than any brief fling could ever be.

Four-and-a-half decades later in Hollywood, that gut feeling was proven to be correct. Ann and I were invited to another *Birdie* premiere. We'd stayed in touch over the years and our paths had crossed on a few occasions, but this reunion was going to be special. The Academy of Motion Picture Arts and Sciences was screening the re-digitized version of the film in April 2011. We both attended the question and answer session afterward, but during the screening, we ducked out of the theater and went to dinner at a Beverly Hills restaurant. There was a lot to catch up on since a twenty-two-year-old Ann-Margret and a twenty-one-year-old me had been lucky enough to be part of a film that people still cared about almost a half-century down the road.

Six months before *Bye Bye Birdie's* April 1963 premiere, we concluded principal photography. The film was finally in the hands of Columbia's editors, marketing staff, and public relations department. I returned home and found a very different Cameo Records. The company I'd known since 1959 seemed to have undergone a radical transformation. But in fact, it had been a gradual one. I just hadn't noticed because I'd always been right in the middle of it. My extended break on the West Coast had allowed me to see things from a fresh perspective.

When Bernie Lowe first signed me, Cameo was a small, two-hit label, whose only successes had been Charlie Gracie's "Butterfly" and a gimmicky 1958 record titled "Dinner with

*My Hollywood reunion with Ann in April of 2011 for the
screening of the re-digitized version of "Birdie."*

Drac" that was recorded by a local TV horror movie host
named John Zacherle. Over the next three years, they upgraded
their recording technology, switching over from monaural to
two-track in 1962. They also hired a full-time engineer named
Joe Tarsia to take some of the pressure off of Dave Appell, who
was now director of A&R. (Six years down the road, Tarsia
would become the legendary engineer and founder of Sigma
Sound Studios.) Concentrating on novelty and dance music,
Bernie and Kal had also signed and recorded a boatload of
new talent. This proved to be a brilliant strategy for Cameo

Waving to the camera with Ernest Evans (better known as Chubby Checker).

that enabled them to seize command of the teenage record market and the weekly Top 10 rankings. Chubby Checker became the face and voice of a national dance obsession with "The Twist" in 1960. The Dovells "Bristol Stomp-ed" across America in '61, and a year later Dee Dee Sharp and then the Orlons "Mashed Potato Time-ed" and "Wah-Watusi-ed" their way to million-selling No. 2 hits.

The company's growing dominance brought about some corporate remodeling. Bernie and Kal merged the individual

Cameo-Parkway Meteoric Climb Only the Beginning, Says Lowe

Pre-Testing Formula Key To C-P Rise

PHILADELPHIA—Two telephone men were completing installation of several direct long-distance telephone lines in the office of Cameo-Parkway's general manager, Harry Chipetz, last week.

One of the men, who was training the other, opened a panel behind Chipetz's desk revealing a jungle of multi-colored wires.

"It wasn't long ago when I came up here to install two phones," the one phoneman said, turning to his companion, "and now look at it—there's just so more room on this panel for any more telephones," he said.

Although a myriad of telephones is not necessarily a legitimate sign of success, it certainly is for Cameo-Parkway. The

PHILADELPHIA — One of the important factors in the success of so many of Cameo-Parkway releases is the label's "pre-testing" formula.

Always changing and updated, the "formula" is based on tight teamwork and communications between top company execs, a.&r. men, promotion men, field men and dealers keyed to keeping up with what's going on around the nation.

Net Earnings Stay Okay

PHILADELPHIA — The Cameo-Parkway financial pic

Bernie Lowe (second from the left) in Cameo-Parkway's headquarters.

Cameo and Parkway labels into one parent label named Cameo-Parkway. Flush with cash, they moved to a much larger facility a few blocks away at 309 South Broad Street. Joe Tarsia (along with an audio technician named Norman Burke) immediately built Cameo two larger, and technologically superior, two-track recording studios at their new address.

So where did I fit in with all of these new developments? If I thought that the answer to that question would come from my next Cameo project, I was dead wrong. Sometimes, the career moves they made on my behalf had me scratching my head and saying, "Huh?" I was a teen idol, right? You'd figure they would have just continued rolling the dice with that formula until it ceased to work anymore, or until I became too long of tooth to be passed off as a seventeen-year-old kid. But not Bernie and Kal. I think sometimes they just threw things at the wall to see if they would stick.

Take *An Era Reborn*, an album I recorded in Los Angeles in 1962. It was a compilation of jazz and big band standards like "Moon River" and "Nice Work If You Can Get It," as well as "Al Di La" and a few other staples from the Italian songbook. I went into the session a little less than thrilled. I would have really dug it if they'd given the record a swingin' Bobby Darin approach, but Cameo had a more traditional Glenn Miller thing in mind.

In spite of what I considered to be their lack of creative thinking, my mood improved dramatically when I viewed the lineup of studio musicians on the floor. It was immediately apparent that Cameo was sparing no expense. Spread out in front of the control booth window was a full big band staffed with cats like Alvin Stoller on drums, bassist Red Mitchell, Frank Rosolino on trombone, and trumpeters Pete Condoli, Conte Condoli, and Conrad Gozzo. In short, it was the dream team, West Coast studio lineup featured on many of Frank Sinatra's biggest Capitol Records hits. I was ecstatic to have all of these musical giants playing on my album, but it was Conrad Gozzo, a legend among horn players because of the fearlessness he routinely displayed in his screaming lead trumpet parts, who captivated my imagination the most.

Conrad was a different breed of trumpet player altogether. I knew the deal when it came to trumpet players' meticulous pre-session preparation habits. They tend to be obsessive about flossing and brushing their teeth before playing, to ensure that food particles wouldn't fly into their mouthpieces. But Conrad had his own, very original preparatory routine.

A few minutes before we were set to begin cutting, he started chomping on a huge Italian hoagie as if he were a great white shark devouring a piece of chum. (You non-Philadelphians probably refer to this delicacy as a *submarine sandwich* or a *hero*.) With oil dripping out of the roll all over the trumpet chart on his music stand, Conrad busied himself with mouthfuls of prosciutto, capicola, provolone, tomatoes, and onions right up until the downbeat. As the conductor signaled that he was ready to count off the tune, Conrad went into his drill. There was a sense of military precision about it. The sequence was:

1. Extract hoagie from jaw.

2. Insert trumpet mouthpiece.

3. Bang out high notes of sufficient power, breadth and fullness to cause the walls of Jericho to come tumbling down.

I'd never seen or *heard* anything like it. I swear, it sounded like a sonic boom was going off in the studio. Besides making me homesick for a South Philly-style sandwich and providing me with a great story that I could pull out of my back pocket during my next musician's hang, *An Era Reborn* did little for my career. But it did make me hunger for a return to the ass-kicking, pop style that had been the backbone of whatever success I'd achieved up until that point. In 1963, that hunger was satisfied when I recorded a tune that took me back to the summers I spent at my grandmother's boarding house down at the shore.

The Dovells had previously recorded a song on the "B" side of their 1963 hit, "You Can't Sit Down," but it was overshadowed by the mega-hit "A" side and didn't get much attention. The song was titled, "Wildwood Days." Bernie Lowe was concentrating on running Cameo-Parkway's business operations at this point and was less involved in the songwriting process. Still, he was the boss, so he was often credited as one of the songwriters on numerous Cameo-Parkway releases from this period—regardless of whether he had written a single note or not. But for some reason, he decided to stay in the background on this tune. Dave Appell, who co-wrote the song with Kal Mann, knew that its potential hadn't been realized with the Dovells, so he decided to try it out on me.

It made sense since everyone knew I was a Wildwood kinda guy. At the very least, my recording session would be a much safer environment for Dave than working with the battling Dovells, who hated each other and were always fighting. If you walked past Cameo's studio and didn't hear someone screaming, "You motherfucker! That's my fuckin' harmony part," it probably wasn't a Dovells session. Dave used to joke that when he walked into a room with them, he needed to bring a whistle and wear a football helmet to break up the fights and protect himself.

Cameo decided to build an entire album around my "Wildwood Days" session and hired an outside-the-company arranger named Steven Garrick, who had arranged hits for Chuck Jackson at New York's Scepter Records. We recorded it at Rec-O-Arts and filled up the rest of the album with new renditions of similar summer beach tunes like "Sea Cruise" and "Moon Over Miami." "Wildwood Days" was a huge regional hit on the East Coast, but it only reached No. 17 on the national charts. The record's limited national appeal was understandable because the city and beaches of Wildwood had no emotional attachment for people out in Iowa and Nebraska, and with La Jolla, Big Sur, Malibu, Santa Monica, and Venice, California had plenty of its own beaches to sing about.

Still, I'm very proud of "Wildwood Days" because of its staying power as a summer party song. It was just a simple, hard-driving shuffle with a percolating organ and a swaggering horn section, but it's been making generations of East Coast folks dance and celebrate for over a half-century. It's even become the official song of Wildwood, New Jersey. If you ever visit, you'll see a huge mural of me right at the corner of Roberts Avenue and the Boardwalk. At my age, it's a beautiful thing to know I'll still be a part of the town I loved as a kid for years to come.

When "Wildwood Days" hit in the summer of '63, I was two years past being a teenager, but Cameo remained committed to pushing the teen idol thing when it came to marketing my records. Don't get me wrong; there are few better feelings for a teenage male than seeing your face plastered across every teen magazine in the country, and knowing you have the power to make legions of cute girls melt in their seats and

*The Roberts Avenue mural of me in Wildwood
commemorating "Wildwood Days."*

scream themselves hoarse whenever you hit the stage. I'm not ungrateful that I was one of the lucky few. Still, there's another side to that story. My numerous shows at Atlantic City's Steel Pier exposed me to both sides of the coin.

This rickety, old entertainment playground stretched more than a quarter of a mile into the ocean. Before the casinos became the new face of Atlantic City, Steel Pier was as identifiable with the town as the Boardwalk and saltwater taffy. From the early 1900s on, generations of Jersey shore patrons grew up exploring the ocean depths in the diving bell, chowing down on junk food, riding the bumper cars, listening to the big bands play their hits, and watching Tony Grant's "Stars of Tomorrow" talent show. And no visit to Steel Pier was complete without a trip to the stadium at the far end to watch the Acapulco cliff divers and the world-famous high-diving horses. It was an incredible sight to see them jump from an elevated platform into a tiny pool of water thirty-five feet below.

But the heart and soul of Steel Pier was the Music Hall Theater, a thousand-seat venue that started out with films and vaudeville shows and eventually evolved into a variety show that featured headlining pop stars like me. On the way to those gigs, it was impossible for me not to be seduced by the car ride down to the shore. The tedious miles of the Black Horse Pike with its signature fruit and produce stands would eventually give way to huge roadside billboards advertising my upcoming Steel Pier dates. As we entered Atlantic City, the two-foot high billboard letters on the Pike that read *"Live In Person, BOBBY RYDELL"* took a backseat to the six-foot high letters on the immense marquee on the side of the pier. Kinda makes a guy feel important, ya know what I mean?

Typically, reality always set in once the actual performing began. Steel Pier may have been fantasyland for Jersey shore vacationers, but for me, it was where I went to work—and I worked *very* hard. Usually, the pier's theater had four or five scheduled shows a day. If I had a hot record on the charts, I would sometimes do as many as *ten*. My days started when a police-escorted limo picked me up early in the morning at my hotel. Having the cops ride shotgun may have seemed like overkill, but I would have been mobbed by fans without them. If I had a few minutes of solitude during the ride, they ended once we drove onto the pier.

My first show started at 10:00 a.m.; the last one ended at 9:00 p.m. Each one followed the same script: I'd be preceded by a

Steel Pier's giant, beachside marquee. At its peak, the pier was 2,298 feet long.

few cartoons or an opening act, and then I did twenty-five to thirty minutes of impersonations, comedy, and sang my hits. Before the final note of the show had died out, I was signing hundreds of autographs in an area just outside of my dressing room while huge lines queued up in front of the theater for the next performance. Eventually, I'd retreat to my dressing room for a few minutes to freshen up, and then a loud buzzer would go off with the five-minute warning before the next show.

Sounds like fun, huh? It was—for maybe the first three or four shows. But from that point on, it became a test of survival. By the fifth or sixth show, numerous members of the house band (usually ten horns and a rhythm section) were completely smashed, courtesy of the bottles and flasks of booze they'd smuggled into the pit to help them get through the repetitive

Either I was about to get arrested for singing off-key, or the officer on my right was stationed there to protect me if any of Steel Pier's more aggressive fans rushed the stage.

drudgery. On occasion, barfing was included at no extra charge.

As each day wore on, lead trumpet player Vic Pace would often settle into two choices of volumes: loud or, *EXTREMELY LOUD!!!* It didn't matter whether the song was an up-tempo tune or a sensitive ballad. By the tenth show, the band probably needed the same cattle prod that was used on the diving horses to get them to finish up the day.

Once in a while, I'd break up the monotony with a short guest appearance on Ed Hurst's TV show, which was broadcast from the pier. The moment I was done, I'd be whisked back to the theater so I could get back on the chain gang. By the end of every Steel Pier run, I was as skinny as a rail. There was never time for anything except performing: no time for girls, no time to rest, and most of all, no time to eat.

Doing my drum thing at Steel Pier as Dave Appell (holding the guitar) looks on. Dave usually conducted my shows there.

If I'd had a theme song to define my existence at the time, it would have been titled, "I hate to bother you while you're eating, but . . ." I've never been one to turn down people for autographs. I was OK—really. My fans gave me the wonderful career I've followed for the last half-century. If they think enough of me that my signature on a piece of paper is going to bring them a little bit of happiness, then I'm more than happy to oblige them. But the constant crowds can have drawbacks.

My friends and family saw it happening but never quite understood it. My cousin Jody used to bug me to go down to the beach at Wildwood with him on the rare occasions in the early '60s when I wasn't working. I finally gave in one day and we picked a semi-secluded spot under the Boardwalk. Within

Signing autographs with Frankie Day looking on.

five to ten minutes, I was engulfed by autograph seekers, general fans, and people who were just curious to see why a crowd had formed. It stayed that way until I went home a few hours later. It wasn't a particularly relaxing afternoon. It was wonderful to be the subject of all the adoration, but it led to a very restrictive life.

I was amazed by Elvis' ability to navigate these waters—at least at the early part of his career—especially since he swam in a much bigger and rougher sea than I did. But back then, the atmosphere was more forgiving. Celebrities could get in trouble, do all kinds of wild, irresponsible things, and usually get away with it. There was an unspoken understanding between the press and police that—unless we did something really stupid and bad—they'd look the other way. People would cover for us.

It's much different today. Elvis and I didn't have the suffocating, nonstop, in-your-face coverage, let alone the social media phenomenon. It makes me a bit more sympathetic than most people in judging the questionable antics of a teen idol like Justin Bieber. As wrong as some of these young stars may be sometimes, it's tough to understand unless you've lived that life.

If I had any serious issues with my teen idol identity, it really wasn't about the lack of privacy or still having to pass myself off as a seventeen-year-old kid, even though I was approaching my twenty-second birthday. No, I could handle all that stuff. My angst was all about the music. My tastes were changing. Don't get me wrong; I still loved rock and roll and pop music, but I was hungry to take on some more ambitious material—like, something that didn't include a "yeah, yeah" or a "whoa, whoa."

In mid-1963 I finally got that opportunity. I'd just finished up a European tour along with a UK pop star named Helen Shapiro, and during a chance meeting, someone presented a song to me composed by a songwriter named Tony Hatch. It was called "Forget Him." Cameo worked out the business details and I recorded it as a sub-contracted deal for PYE records, a UK label that was an RCA subsidiary known for artists like Lonnie Donegan, the early Kinks, and Petula Clark.

Bernie Lowe wasn't wild about releasing the record in the States. Because the song hadn't been composed by Lowe,

Mann, or Appell, Cameo wouldn't get any publishing revenues. CHUM radio out of Toronto took the decision out of his hands by broadcasting the track in heavy rotation. When "Forget Him" became a huge hit up in Canada, Bernie finally relented and released the record in the U.S.

I didn't know it at the time, but this was my peak as a recording artist. It was the most clout I'd ever have in my recording career. "Forget Him" was my last million-seller, topping out at No. 4 on the pop charts. I was making five cents on every 45 sold—a ridiculously low amount of financial compensation by today's standards, but a hefty sum for the early '60s. Soon enough, it would all end and seem almost insignificant.

There were no warning signs of Cameo-Parkway's imminent decline and demise. In fact, 1963 was a banner year for the label: Chubby Checker had half a dozen Top 40 songs, the Orlons' "South Street" peaked at No. 3, and so did the Dovell's "You Can't Sit Down." Dee Dee Sharp had a Top 10 hit with "Do The Bird" and rookie act, the Tymes, started their Cameo career with the chart topping, one-for-the-ages hit, "So Much In Love." My contribution to this seemingly unstoppable conveyor belt of hits was the aforementioned "Wildwood Days" and "Forget Him."

In less than a year, the walls of 309 South Broad St. shook down to the building's foundation. But not because Georgie

Young and the Rockin' Bocs were pumping out sledgehammer beats in the studio, or because the Dovells were in the midst of one of their signature slugfests. This shock wave came from the United Kingdom by way of New York City.

Earlier in the year, in the midst of the European tour with Helen Shapiro, we'd just finished a show in London and our tour bus was about to take off, when a car pulled in front of us. A guy stepped out of the car, knocked on the bus' door and asked if I would meet with an upcoming band he had with him. It was a quartet. I had no idea who they were—they had no major hit records in the States at the time—but they seemed nice enough. It was all over within five minutes. I have no recollection of what we talked about.

I'm sure you guessed that the "upcoming band" was the Beatles, and the guy who knocked on my tour bus door was most likely their manager Brian Epstein. Eight months later on February 9th, 1964, I stared at my television set in disbelief as they sang "I Want To Hold Your Hand" on *The Ed Sullivan Show*. If I'd known what the repercussions of that performance would be, maybe I would have locked John, Paul, George, and Ringo in the bathroom of my bus or stolen their instruments out of the trunk of their car.

It wouldn't have made any difference though. The Beatles were the locomotive of a runaway train that was soon bowling over everything in its path. They spearheaded a British invasion that ended American pop music as we knew it. Motown, Stax, and R&B in general survived, but most mainstream, white boy acts like mine hit a brick wall. (The Beach Boys and the

On stage in London.

Four Seasons were among the few homegrown U.S. pop acts that escaped the slaughter.) Nobody wanted to hear us on the radio anymore. All the DJs were interested in playing was the Beatles, the Stones, Herman's Hermits, the Animals, Freddie and the Dreamers, the Dave Clark Five, and any other UK group that sported mop-top haircuts and a Brit accent.

Later in 1964, I had a shot at hopping on board the train, but we blew it. I recorded a Paul McCartney tune titled, "A World Without Love" in a bombastic Dave Appell arrangement that we cut in New York City at A&R studios. Vocally, it was as strong a track as I'd ever belted out and it got me thinking that maybe I was going to finally land my first No. 1 pop hit. A month or so later on one of my frequent road trips to and from New York, Frankie Day and I were listening to Cousin Brucie on WABC when he played "A World Without Love." Frankie went absolutely berserk, unleashing a quintuple X-rated tirade. It wasn't my version; it was one by a new act—a British one, naturally—called Peter and Gordon.

I'd been scooped. My recording of the song wasn't due to come out for another two weeks. Cameo had putzed around and taken too much time in getting it released. It was the arrogance of a giant that didn't realize it was on the verge of being brought down by a mosquito—a previously unknown group's first single—and it wasn't the first time. Bernie Lowe had dismissed the Beatles as a "passing fad" when they were initially offered to Cameo-Parkway in 1963.

Paul McCartney had composed the song when he was just sixteen, but never felt it was strong enough for the

Beatles. Much to my bad fortune, he eventually gave it to Peter Asher, the brother of his then-girlfriend Jane Asher. Back in Philadelphia, my version of "A World Without Love" charted as a No. 1 record, but on the national scene, it never cracked the Top 40. Peter and Gordon's record? It took No. 1 honors both in the UK and in *Billboard's* Top 100 chart in the U.S.

That was the beginning of the end for me at Cameo. I recorded a few more inconsequential tracks for them throughout 1964, but it wouldn't have mattered much if they'd hit or not. The downward spiral that was beginning for Cameo-Parkway wasn't really about me, the British Invasion, or even the loss of the label's principal promotional tool when *American Bandstand* relocated that same year to Los Angeles. This was all about Bernie Lowe.

At heart, he was just a musician, a good guy who, through hard work, some luck, and impeccable timing, found himself holding the reins of a world-class thoroughbred that was a money-making machine. Bernie had always detested the business side of the operation, and as time went on, he became more and more depressed and insecure about his ability to keep Cameo humming atop the charts. When everything was going his way, those personality deficiencies were just a minor annoyance to those around him (namely Dave Appell and Kal Mann). But when record sales dramatically dropped off and *American Bandstand* departed, Bernie no longer had the energy or vision to fight his way back to the top of the heap. His heart just wasn't in it anymore.

Cameo made a few half-assed attempts at answering the Brit problem, including "A World Without Love" with its botched marketing. They released an early Kinks single and another by ex-Beatle Pete Best. But regardless of how good or bad these tracks were, they were doomed by the label's ineffective counterpunches. Even worse were Cameo's pathetic attempts to enter the growing soul music marketplace.

The one modest success in its group of R&B releases offered a preview of Philadelphia's future recording scene. Candy & The Kisses' single, "The 81," never cracked the Top 40, but it was composed by a young Cameo songwriter named Kenny Gamble, and the "B" side was penned by one of their studio musicians named Leon Huff. Less than a decade later, the two of them founded Philadelphia International Records and ruled the R&B world after knocking Motown off of the throne it had held throughout the '60s.

Dave Appell departed in 1964 and Bernie Lowe resigned as president of Cameo the following year. The label was quickly sold, and within three years, its stock was de-listed because of continued heavy financial losses. By early 1969, it ceased to exist at all. It was now called ABKCO Industries and was run and owned by the Beatles' former manager, Allen Klein, who sat on the Cameo catalog for the next four decades and did nothing with it. The only place you could buy a Bobby Rydell record during all that time was in a used record bin at a second-hand shop.

In late 1964, just before the label descended into the abyss, I amicably parted ways with Bernie and Kal. It was far from being a desperate "What is going to happen to me now?" situation. I'd just finished up a five-year period that had generated fourteen albums, thirty-four charted hits (seventeen of which were Top 40 and seven of which were Top 10), five gold records, and even though I'd narrowly missed that elusive No. 1 hit ("Volare" was a No. 2), I still sold 25 million records. Some record label was going to make me an offer. Besides, with a schedule packed with bookings, I had the luxury of taking my time before I made my next recording career decision.

Many of those commitments were TV appearances on variety and talk shows like *Shindig!* and *The Mike Douglas Show* out of Philadelphia, but my fondest memory from that period was an acting gig on the hit television series *Combat!* Vic Morrow, the show's star, was a real pro. He was a damn good actor and a joy to work with. Tragically, he was killed in 1982, decapitated by a helicopter blade during the filming of the 1982 movie *The Twilight Zone*. The *Combat!* episode I worked on was titled, "The Duel," and was one of the series' mostly highly acclaimed shows. I played an Army truck driver who, while trying to fix a flat tire, became pinned under the truck. Vic, in his role as Sgt. Saunders, protected me by singlehandedly taking on a German tank.

I didn't know it at the time, but that lone *Combat!* appearance would offer me a huge opportunity several years later. Lynn Stalmaster, the award-winning casting director who had hired me, was impressed with my performance and recommended me for an important role in a new movie that was being directed by Mike Nichols. It was called *The Graduate*. I read for the

Singing with Mike Douglas.

part and made it to the final rounds, but they were going for a new face with more of a disheveled, college kid look. Besides, it was doubtful that I had the acting chops to dislodge someone of the caliber of Dustin Hoffman.

But I did have the *singing* chops to get a quick offer from a major label. Not just any label, but Capitol—Capitol *friggin'* Records!! Excuse my French, and with all due respect, forget the Beatles being on this label; I was more thrilled that I was going to be on the same label that Frank Sinatra recorded for during his heyday. Within a few months of leaving Cameo, I signed with them. Over a two-year period, I recorded twenty-five songs and released several singles and an album titled

On the set of the hit TV series, "Combat!" sometime around 1963 or '64.

Somebody Loves You, but regrettably, nothing much happened and the relationship ended in 1966.

Capitol was going after a more easy listening, adult approach that included some Cynthia Weil-Barry Mann and Gerry Goffin-Carole King tunes. None of them resonated with my audience, although my 1965 version of Paul Anka's "Diana" did break into *Billboard's* Top 100. It was a takeoff on the Righteous Brothers' version of "Ebb Tide," as opposed to the song's original quasi-rhumba feel with Paul. It had a shot at making some noise, but just as it was gaining momentum, Capitol switched its promotional weight over to Wayne Newton's "Red Roses for a Blue Lady." So much for the high of being on the same label as the Chairman of the Board.

Recording a vocal track at Capitol Records.

But in early 1968, a few years after my disappointing result at Capitol, I was signed by Reprise Records, the label Frank founded in 1960. I was knocked out when I was told he personally wanted me on their artist roster. My first Reprise session started out on a high note when we cut a promising track titled "It's Getting Better," and then a second one called "The River Is Wide." Glen Campbell was working as a studio guitarist on the date and said to me afterwards, "Bobby, it looks like you're going to be back on the charts." But, the day's initial exhilaration faded in the coming weeks; Reprise did very little with either tune. The Grass Roots had better luck with one of the songs when they hit with "The River Is Wide." The rest of my Reprise output didn't fare any better. As with Capitol, my new record deal proved to be a short-lived one.

I didn't blame Frank. He will always be one of the two most important heroes and role models in my life. The Hoboken native was the embodiment of everything that was cool, stylish, suave, and Italian. My other hero was an egotistical, brash, loudmouth Jewish cat from Brooklyn, who also happened to be a good friend of mine.

I first met Buddy Rich in the early '60s at Birdland in New York City. Lou Spencer, the guy who choreographed my act when I debuted at the Copa, was old friends with Buddy. Almost from the first moment Lou introduced us, we hit it off. Starstruck teenager that I was, I asked for his autograph. Buddy warmly shook my hand, looked me right in the eyes and told me, "Kid, this is worth much more than an autograph."

Come to think of it, it really was worth more. Buddy wasn't the easiest guy to get close to. He was capable of great warmth and generosity, but he had a volcanic, and sometimes uncontrollable, temper. (Just ask any member of his bands over the years.) He was also consumed with an insatiable need to be No. 1, especially when it came to playing drums. He was the Ty Cobb of the music world.

I learned this one night in Los Angeles in 1966, four or five years after we first met. I was in town for a week preparing for an appearance on Milton Berle's TV Show. Buddy was in his *West Side Story Medley* period, and he and his band were in the middle of a lengthy run at a club called The Chez. I caught his act every night for a week straight, and on my last night in town, he singled me out to the audience and gave me a great buildup, telling everyone, "Not only is Bobby a great singer, but he's also one helluva drummer." Then he surprised me by asking me to come onstage and sit in.

Buddy had been blowing me away all week with a tune called "New Blue," and after hearing him play it six nights in a row, I knew it inside out. I counted it off for the band and then flat-out nailed it. I was making all the rhythmic hits and fills and really hamming it up. The crowd really got into it and rewarded me with a loud round of applause.

Naturally, that went right up Buddy's ass. *Nobody* upstages Buddy Rich. As the applause died down, he threw a tough Louie Bellson chart on the stand and told me, "Play this one." The tune had a breakneck tempo and some very tricky four-bar drum breaks. I knew I was in for it but gave it my best shot. I was doing OK until the sticks flew out of my hands during one of the breaks and clattered on to the stage. I looked over at Buddy and the ball-busting prick was doubled over, laughing his ass off. I'd been put in my place.

In a small way, I eventually got him back. A few years later, we were hanging out at the Monterey Jazz Festival. One of the acts was an avant-garde saxophonist—probably someone like Ornette Coleman or Anthony Braxton—who was playing all kinds of crazy shit. It was a foreign language to Buddy, who bitched," What kind of fuckin' music are they playin'? I don't have the slightest clue what they're doing. Where's the melody?"

Putting on a condescending air, I lectured him: "I can't believe you don't recognize that song, Buddy. He's playing 'Stardust.'" Buddy looked puzzled for a moment, and I could tell he was listening intently and trying to recognize that melody in the avalanche of notes the guy was playing. I must have done a lousy job of keeping a straight face because he quickly figured out I was messing with him. "Fuck you, Rydell," he snorted and immediately went back to complaining about the music. It was a minor bit of cheap revenge for me, but I still dug the moment.

For most people, the old adage about talent being overrated is usually true. Successful entertainers are usually a combination of talent, hard work, and some outside positive reinforcement along the way. Once-in-a-lifetime musicians like Buddy Rich are the exception. Sure, he practiced until his hands bled when he was young, but so did a lot of other musicians. Only a tiny handful of them ever reached genius status like Buddy. He's one of those rare people that God touches on the forehead and says, "Tag, you're it."

Buddy didn't need anyone pumping him up; his oversized ego was bulletproof and impervious to the occasional bouts of self-doubt that plague most of us. Me? I've always been a very confident performer because I knew I had the goods.

My vocal chops were a gift, but my overall musicianship was formed by seriously studying the phrasing and breathing of Frank Sinatra, Tony Bennett, and other great singers. Playing drums also played a huge role because I developed a strong sense of time along the way. I could lay back, ride on top of the beat, or play it right down the middle.

I also had wonderful people in my corner who built up my self-image. My Dad was a bottomless well of positivity, as was Frankie Day. In 1965 I hired a new conductor named Rocky Valentine who also encouraged me on an almost daily basis. I'd known Rocky since I was ten. He used to play trumpet at the Earle Theater, but I first met him when he was leading the band at Eddie Suez's Club Avalon. Rocky was a very classy guy—a dead ringer for Rudolph Valentino. I have no idea where he picked it up, but he spoke with a very distinct Italian accent and he always called me "King." Not a bad thing to hear when you've just been released by two labels in a row.

I previously stated that I've never suffered from stage fright. I still stand by that statement, but nervousness? That's a different animal. They're the same thing you say? Not really. To me, stage fright is a general fear of performing in front of a lot of people. Nervousness—in a show business context—is more of a specific concern about something that's difficult to perform or a weakness in your skill set. If one aspect in my talent arsenal gave me some doubts, it was dancing. I was fine with the dance

In my hotel room before a show, going over the details of a new arrangement with Carl Mottola (left) and my new conductor Rocky Valentine (center).

sequences I performed in *Bye Bye Birdie*. In fact, I thought I did a terrific job, but as choreography goes, it wasn't anywhere near as demanding as my next musical.

I was playing the role of Riff in a summer stock production of *West Side Story*. That meant I had to learn some of the original dance routines conceived by legendary choreographer Jerome Robbins. Right from the start of rehearsals, I was struggling with the steps, particularly the solo I had on a song called "Cool." It wasn't the first time that the dancing demands of that role humbled an actor. I called Frankie Day and told him I was worried about my ability to pull it off. "You'll do it and you'll be great," he responded, half chiding me and half pumping up my confidence.

After busting my ass for the next few weeks with the show's dance coach, we opened in Columbus, Ohio. The following day, I called my Dad and said, "You gotta come out here, I'm fuckin' great!" Quite a turnaround from the whiny, doubting Thomas I was a few weeks before.

Emotional ups and downs go with the territory if you perform in the public eye and have a lengthy career. Not everyone can handle the weight of their career disappointments. Just think about the Red Sox's Bill Buckner or Florence Ballard of the Supremes and how they had failures in the spotlight that wrecked their lives. In Bill's case, it lasted for a few decades; for Florence, it was forever. I've been fortunate that my internal makeup has kept me from celebrating my successes too much, and helped me to quickly brush off my defeats. I lick my wounds and move on to the next challenge. But that doesn't mean that I don't have career regrets.

In the early '80s, I was offered Robert Klein's role (and the opportunity to co-star with Lucie Arnaz) in Neil Simon's hit musical *They're Playing Our Song* after Onna White, the choreographer on *Bye Bye Birdie,* had recommended me for the part. I went to see the show, but came away unimpressed. I turned down the offer because the producers couldn't guarantee that the show would remain in New York. It was a dumb move. The show continued to be a hit for years and could have opened a lot of doors for me.

That boneheaded decision stayed with me for a long time, but to show you how I always think like a kid, my toughest disappointment didn't involve my career; it was over a set of drums. I was very attached to the set of black Ludwig drums that my dad bought me when I was a teenager. I have no idea why, but one day I lost my mind when I saw a shiny, blue pearl set of Rogers drums, and I immediately traded my Ludwigs for them. Within days, I realized I hated the new drums. They were a pain in the ass to set up and didn't sound as good as the Ludwigs. But there was nothing I could do about it. The deal was done.

A lot of Italian singers from my era—and probably a decade or two before—were rumored to have mob affiliations or mob backing. The stories of Frank Sinatra's alleged connections to guys like Sam Giancana and Vito Genovese dogged him throughout his career. Everyone knew how close he was with Paul "Skinny" D'Amato, who ran Atlantic City's 500 Club, a place that was known far and wide as a popular back-room hangout for organized crime figures. But if any of us Italian crooners wanted to distance ourselves from the image of a mob-backed Italian singer, it became almost impossible after my fellow South Philadelphian, Al Martino, played Johnny Fontane in *The Godfather*. From then on, everybody just took it for granted: "Oh, you're a big Italian singing star; you must have the Mafia behind you."

Now if you're looking for some juicy "wise-guy" gossip, I'm sorry, but I'll have to disappoint you. Maybe it was because my level of stardom was not as big as Sinatra's, but for whatever reason, the mob never put much of an effort into muscling in on my action. . . . . By your silence, I can tell you're skeptical. OK, OK. I'll throw you a few titillating scraps. I certainly met, and knew, my share of "the boys." Until casino gaming commissions cracked down on them, they flocked to gambling and entertainment meccas like Las Vegas and Atlantic City. But as much as they may have wanted to get in on the underworld financial action those environments offered, there was also an innocent side to their addiction to casino life. The lights, the glamour, beautiful women, fancy clothes, and the perceived sophistication of the overall scene, where great singers were belting out tunes in front of ass-kicking big bands—it was all an irresistible, integral part of mob tradition.

Often when I was performing at nightclubs and casinos, the guys would be around, just digging the music and socializing with their wives or goomahs. Like if I played Palumbo's in South Philly, Nicky Scarfo, Philip Testa, or several of the other local Philly boys might be hanging at the bar. We might have a drink together, tell a few jokes or talk sports, but that's as far as it ever went. The same type of thing happened to me at lots of other venues around the country. But one mid-'60s appearance at the Latin Quarter in New York did give me a more personal look into the social culture of what many, rightly or wrongly, perceive to be organized crime.

The maitre d' at the club told me that someone by the name of "Louie D" wanted to meet me, and that he was someone I should definitely want to get to know. Up walks this very dapper-looking gentleman oozing power and charisma. I was impressed at first sight. Louie looked me right in the eyes, firmly shook my hand and said, "I don't know what it is about you kid, but I love you." Jesus, who could ask for a better start to a relationship than that? I asked around and was told Louie owned a restaurant called Separate Tables and supposedly was connected with the Gambino family. I surmised he had some serious pull in certain unspecified circles.

Frankly, I didn't give a crap about whether he was connected or not—except in the case of *one* of his particular relationships. I was hanging out one night with Louie, Frankie Day, and Carl Mottola at the Sands in Las Vegas, when—in a scene reminiscent of a night at the Copa five years earlier—who comes walking through the lobby but Frank Sinatra with his wife Mia Farrow and Joe E. Lewis. Sinatra makes a beeline for Louie, gives him a big hug and kisses him on the cheek. Then we all headed off to the lounge for a few drinks. Remembering me from our previous meeting six years earlier, Frank asked me, "So what have you been doing with yourself, Robert?" I told him I still had my usual schedule of recordings and nightclub concerts, and that I was currently up for a role in a Disney film. Frank shook his head and said, "You'll never get it." I was taken aback and replied, "Excuse me?" "You're Italian," he said. "That's why you aren't going to get it." I wasn't about to question him or point out Annette Funicello's steady employment with Disney over the years. Besides, he proved to be right. I *didn't* get the part.

Eventually we all followed Frank down to the casino floor and watched him stand behind a dealer and conduct a blackjack game. (You can do that when you're Frank Sinatra.) It looked like he was going to be there for quite a while, and since I had a show to do, I excused myself. As I started to walk away, he said, "Goodnight, Robert," then paused for a moment and added, "Goodnight Carlooch," to my drummer. Carl Mottola almost had a heart attack. Like me, he idolized Sinatra. He was shocked that Frank even remembered his name, let alone was honoring him by referring to him as "Carlooch," a nickname of endearment for Italians named Carl.

A few months later in New York, I had dinner with Louie and two of his "associates" in Little Italy. I'm pretty sure they were his bodyguards. We were having a great time talking about the usual stuff—food, music, women—and he also asked me a few questions about my career. After a short pause, he got all serious on me and said, "Bobby, you know Sinatra loves you." "I love him, too," I replied, not really knowing where he was going with this line of conversation. Then Louie delivered an unexpected and unwanted critique: "You should be much bigger than you are. I think your father fucked up your career."

My spine instantly tightened up and I saw red. Looking him right in the eye, I said, "Louie, you're a fuckin' liar." As soon as the words left my mouth, I knew I was in trouble. Louie pounded his fist on the table and walked away, leaving me with his two associates. Their friendly demeanor of ten seconds earlier turned menacing and they said, "Are you fuckin' crazy? That man you just called a liar—do you know who that is?"

My temples were pounding and my head was racing. I thought I'd either just ended my career or even worse, I was gonna get whacked. After an agonizingly uncomfortable minute of silence, Louie returned to the table, smiled, gave me a hug and kissed me on the cheek. I think it was an Italian thing. I guess he had respected me for being a man by standing up for my pop.

Maybe he was feeling me out for Frank or the boys downtown, and maybe I'd have been a bigger star if I let them handle me; maybe not. I'll never know. Some mob guys had approached Frankie Day several times during that same era about getting involved with my career. Frankie just politely declined the offer each time. Pretty innocent stuff. Nobody ever pressured or threatened us. As for Louie, we remained good friends, but we never talked about my career again.

Shortly before he passed away a few years later, he bailed me out of a big jam when I was appearing at the Lion's Den in the Las Vegas MGM Grand. I'd been gambling all week and losing badly—like, to the tune of thirty grand. I didn't even have enough cash left to pay my hotel bill or buy my airline ticket home. Not knowing where to turn for help, I called Louie. After a brief, fatherly lecture that began with "Bobby, what'd you do?" he said, "Look, I'm gonna wire you three thousand bucks and I'm not gonna charge you no juice. But I want the money back as soon as you get home." Believe me, I took care of that debt quicker than you could say *pasta fagioli*. I never knew what Louie did in his behind-the-scenes business dealings, but I do know that all I ever saw was a caring, honorable man. I have nothing but fond memories of him.

That wasn't the first time that an alleged mob figure helped me out of a tough situation. In 1969, I landed a role in an Australian spy film called *That Lady from Peking* which also starred Carl Betz and Nancy Kwan. I was still red hot Down Under, so Eddie Davis, the director, was probably trying to boost the film's appeal by capitalizing on my popularity. We were scheduled to shoot in Sydney in July.

It looked like a great gig except for one major complication; right in the middle of the shooting schedule, I had a date on the books to appear at the Americana Hotel in Miami. The club's owner wouldn't let me out of the booking and was threatening a lawsuit if I breached the contract. Frankie Day was trying to convince him to reschedule the show, arguing that the film would enhance my career and guarantee him an even bigger draw when I returned. The Americana's owner wasn't buying it; he wouldn't budge.

At the time all this behind-the-scenes drama was unfolding, I was in North Wildwood at my grandmother's place taking in some R&R before I had to fly ten thousand miles to Australia. Not far away in Wildwood Crest was a place called the Suntan Motel, owned by a friend of mine named Charlie Notto and his wife, Helen. My dad and I went over one day to visit, and who should be sitting by the pool large-as-life but Angelo Bruno, the reputed head of the Philadelphia mob. My dad recognized him immediately from all the pictures that had been running in the Philadelphia *Bulletin* and the *Inquirer,* and struck up a conversation with him. After telling him of my recent plight with the scheduling conflict, Angelo replied that he might be able to help.

Now I know what you're thinking: Here comes the stereo-typical "offer you can't refuse," the severed horse head in the bed, and all the other usual suspects. But believe it or not, it was all pretty tame. Angelo knew people in Miami who had connections to the club owner. All it took was a few phone calls, and I had a rescheduled date at the club. I was free to fly to Australia. No money exchanged, no one roughed up, no follow-up obligations; just an act of kindness by a man who liked my father and my music.

Too bad Mr. Bruno didn't offer his considerable abilities to lean on some of the film critics. When *That Lady from Peking* was finally released several years later, they panned it. The film was a critical and commercial flop.

THE BRIDGE

Throughout all the years of hits, concerts, TV appearances, movies, and changes of record labels, there was only one constant in my life: my Camille. We'd been dating forever, although it wasn't dating in the traditional sense. We didn't go out on the town or frequent movies or restaurants—at least not until some years later. We just spent a lot of time together. When "Kissin' Time" broke into the charts, everything changed. My newfound success kept me on the road and away from her for extended periods of time. I couldn't even take her to her senior high school prom because I was on tour in Australia.

There was also another reason why the basic nature of our relationship changed. My early recording career was fueled by whatever fantasy and sex appeal I represented to teenage girls. Because of this, Frankie Day believed that any hint that I was

Me and my childhood sweetheart Camille.

romantically unavailable would have translated into decreased record sales and diminished box office receipts at my live shows. To keep up the facade that I was single, Frankie made it clear that Camille had to stay in the background. Whenever she came to one of my performances, she was always introduced as a cousin or a family friend.

I don't know how she put up with it . . . well, actually, I do. Aside from having the patience of a saint, Camille was extremely confident and very brainy. She was never scared of losing me to my career, and was able to look far down the road and see the bigger picture. In her mind, she felt secure in our relationship as long as she was the one I left with at the end of the day. But, the place we'd go to when we did leave was about to change.

You'd have never known I was a star. Yeah, when I first hit, I bought myself a few trinkets that were out of reach for the average Joe. There was a coral-colored Pontiac Bonneville after I made a few bucks from "Kissin' Time." Then I graduated to a gold Lincoln Continental a year or two later, and a Corvette Stingray a few years after that.

But Frankie Day and my mother still picked out my clothes, and I was still living with my parents in my grandparents' tiny row home. How could I have any kind of serious relationship with Camille under those conditions?

The success of "Forget Him" in 1963 solved those problems. I moved my parents, grandparents, and myself out of South Philly and into a new home in suburban Penn Valley. Instead of the short walk around the corner to see Camille,

My prized Corvette, outside my grandmother's house in Wildwood.

the new lifeline of our relationship was a ten-mile car ride on the Schuykill Expressway. I'd started driving when I was eighteen, but my mother didn't want a novice like me navigating a hazardous road that had been nicknamed the Sure-kill Expressway. To placate her fears, my dad had the job of shuttling me back and forth to the old neighborhood every time I wanted to see Camille. We'd spend a few hours together and then he'd drive me back to Penn Valley.

It was a workable, comfortable relationship for both of us because Camille wasn't a typical South Philly girl. She never pressured me about getting married, and when we finally

G.I. Bobby in Indiana, PA.

did get around to discussing tying the knot, it felt like a natural progression of the love we felt for each other. When Dan Quattrone asked me, "Are you ever going to marry my daughter?" I didn't mind. He was just being a protective father who wanted to make sure she hadn't invested ten of the prime years of her life and come out with nothing. I reassured him as best as I could despite a busy, unpredictable schedule that was getting even busier.

I started a stint in the National Guard in 1964 that began with two months of basic training at Fort Dix. I'd been transformed from Bobby Rydell, pompadoured teen idol making thousands of dollars a week, to Pvt. Robert L. Ridarelli, a low ranking soldier with a crew cut making $85 a month. Once

Basic training at Fort Dix, NJ, sometime around late 1964 or early 1965.

Getting ready to fly to Vietnam. From left to right: Frankie Day, DJ Georgie Woods, me surrounded by two of the dancers, Carl Mottola, and Jimmy Wisner.

basic training ended, I had to serve one weekend every month at the armory for the next six years. On the off-weeks, I toured, but the road now felt different. Every time I left—especially when I went outside the U.S.—I missed Camille more and more.

One of the tougher periods occurred in February 1966 when I toured South Vietnam for three weeks. Accompanied by Philly DJ Georgie Woods ("the guy with the goods"), a few dancing girls, and a trio that featured Carl Mottola on drums, Frankie Day on bass, and jazz keyboardist Jimmy Wisner playing accordion, we flew out on a military transport on January 30th and arrived 9,000 miles later at Tan Son Nhut air base.

Singing for the troops in Vietnam.

This was no Bob Hope tour. We hit Saigon, Da Nang, and other large cities, but we also spent a lot of time flying out in helicopters and traveling in tanks to reach troops in the more remote areas and jungles of Vietnam. I liked it that way. The generals and colonels wanted me to hobnob with them in their officer's clubs behind the front lines, but I preferred being with the grunts who were in the middle of all the action. I *was* one of them, wasn't I? Even though I was in the National Guard as opposed to the Army or Marines, I was still just a low-level soldier like them, so we related to each other.

At outposts surrounded by sandbags and soldiers with M60s, I slept on cots with loaded guns and hand grenades less than an arm's-length away. In Kon Tum, I sang "What Kind of Fool

I felt more comfortable with the grunts in the field than with the Army brass.

Am I?" to a large crowd of Marines while howitzers were laying down a barrage a few miles away. "Don't worry, that's outgoing, not incoming," one Marine told me. Like that was supposed to put me at ease? In spite of all the protection around the band and me, a well-placed mortar shell fired by the Vietcong would have rendered all of it useless. I heard similar artillery shelling in the distance on an almost daily basis. I visited horribly wounded soldiers—most of them just teenagers—in hospitals and makeshift MASH units. It was heartbreaking. My run of Top 40 hits and concert tours suddenly seemed far away and insignificant; life seemed very short. I figured it was time.

On one of my National Guard weekends in 1967, I was dismissed early from my duties, so I decided to surprise

Camille. It was her birthday and she was celebrating at a restaurant on the Delaware River with her sister and some friends. I barged in wearing my fatigues and combat boots. It wasn't a down-on-my-knees moment, but I proposed and gave her an engagement ring. Since my teen idol days were now in the rearview mirror, Frankie Day was OK with it and happy for both of us. Still, realizing that being Mrs. Bobby Rydell would thrust Camille into the public eye, he sent her to a finishing school for six months. I didn't see the need for it. To me, she was fine just the way she was, but Camille didn't seem to mind.

We finally got married on October 5, 1968 at Stella Maris Church in South Philly. I woke the next morning to see a front-page picture in the Philadelphia *Inquirer* of Camille and me walking down the steps of the church with close to one thousand of my fans in the street throwing rice at us as we entered a Rolls-Royce Silver Phantom limo. We did it up right with a beautiful reception at the Warwick Hotel, and then left the next morning for a honeymoon in Hawaii.

At the time, everyone flew TWA. I always got a kick out of checking in at the Philadelphia airport because I'd gotten to know a guy there named Tommy who was the head skycap. I'd taken so many flights over the years that we'd become good friends. Tommy had wall-to-wall personality and was very popular with all the celebrities who came through town, particularly Sinatra. He made a ton of money on tips. He had heard about my wedding, so when he saw me pull up to the terminal with Camille, he took one look at her and said to me, "Hey, Mr. Rydell, I see you married a *sis-tah*." I laughed and

With my parents and Camille at her wedding shower.

Our wedding photo.

told him Camille was really white, but he wouldn't hear it. It was easy to see why; she had dark olive skin, and there were still remnants of her summer tan.

I had a week-and-a-half of lying on Hawaii's beaches to catch up to her melanin level. Our honeymoon couldn't have been better. Of course, we went to Don Ho's and he dragged me up on stage to sing "Volare." Hawaii was a great way to start our marriage, and our stay there was a much needed opportunity to clear my head. I had a major career decision to make when I got back home.

Upon our return, Camille moved into what was now *our* Penn Valley home and set up housekeeping. She wasted no

Camille in the kitchen with my grandmother and mother.

time in becoming the world's second-greatest Italian cook. My grandmother was the first, so with the close relationship she had with Camille, all those great recipes had a smooth transition into the next generation of Ridarellis. In typical Old World Italian style, Grandmom Lena died less than a year later. Content with the knowledge that her life's recipes were in good hands, she was able to let go and move on. Not to be outdone in the tradition department, my grandfather died a year later to be with his wife.

Once things got back to normal, Camille set out to establish her own identity within the house. As for me, I was preoccupied with whether or not we'd remain in the house in the first place. For several years, friends, colleagues, agents, and Frankie Day had all floated the idea that I should relocate to the West Coast. An appearance on *The Tonight Show* had reinforced the notion. With all the TV work I was doing there, and its proximity to Las Vegas, Los Angeles seemed like the logical place for me to be. The past six or seven years had taught me that I brought a lot more to the table than the average pop star. Besides singing rock and roll and pop music, I could croon or belt a jazz standard with a big orchestra; I could play an instrument with a high level of proficiency, and having knocked it out of the park on a major motion picture and dozens of TV appearances, I firmly believed in my ability to act, handle comedy roles, and even dance.

Yet, in the end, I opted to stay a Philly guy. Over the years, people have said it was a bad career move and that my parents talked me out of it. I disagree with the first notion and the second one is crap. It was my decision and no one else's. Maybe living in the hub of the entertainment business in Los Angeles would have pushed my career into the stratosphere, but how big did I have to be? I already couldn't go out in public without being mobbed, and even after the glory days of '59 through '64 were a thing of the past, I was still out on the road five or six months every year. All my friends and family were in Philadelphia. I didn't want to root for the Dodgers, Rams, Lakers, and Kings (I was a die-hard fan of the Phillies, the Eagles, the 76ers, and

Singing the National Anthem at a Philadelphia Eagles game.

the Flyers), and I wanted my wife and me to have kids and raise them in the same town where we both grew up. For better or worse, I've never regretted the decision to stay put.

Throughout my career, I've never really had to stress out or become depressed over a lack of work. Even without any new hit records or TV appearances, I always knew I could work as long as I wanted because I was confident in my vocal chops and overall talent. I got through the late '60s and early '70s by playing rock and roll revival shows at Madison Square Garden and appearing regularly on the hotel and nightclub circuits

147

of the Waldorf, the Hyatt Regency, Hugh Hefner's Playboy Clubs, and Disney theme parks. I even appeared in a summer stock production of *Bye Bye Birdie*, this time as Kim's father, instead of the Hugo Peabody role.

Still, if I had to pick a down period, it would be the decade of the early '70s through the early '80s. It certainly started out well enough. Of all the artists who played at Steel Pier since its 1898 debut, I was the one chosen to play its last show in 1971. The same year, the hit Broadway show, *Grease,* opened with a storyline set in a fictional high school coincidentally named "Rydell High." Both events were nice boosts for my ego, but neither of them was going to get me any additional work.

Don't get me wrong. It wasn't like I was unemployed or anything like that. But I was shifting gears as fast as I could: fewer concerts and casino showrooms, more private gigs and cruise ships. I wouldn't exactly call it slumming. Royal Caribbean took great care of me with bookings on the *Sovereign of the Seas*—two shows, two nights a week, on seven-day cruises for a very healthy payday. I wasn't merely making the best of things; I was thriving. On my off days, I'd usually head to one of the lounges to sit in and sing jazz and pop standards with the pianist. I made a habit of staying until 2:00 a.m. and keeping the joint packed until closing time. The cruise line loved me because these impromptu appearances generated a lot of unexpected income for them.

The significant changes in my work schedule meant that I got to spend more time at home than I had in years. The timing couldn't have been better. Camille had given birth to our son,

Robert and Jennifer.

Robert, on September 1st, 1969, and our daughter, Jennifer, was born four-and-a-half years later on February 20th, 1974. During the kids' infancies, Camille had to handle way too many of the child-rearing responsibilities because I was always out on the road. It was high time for me to do my share.

I was finally around to see Robert and Jennifer grow up. We did the Disney World thing, took vacations and did homework together, and in time, I developed a new identity for myself: suburban soccer mom. I drove the kids to all their athletic events and got involved with their teams. I was the first base coach for Robert's Little League team, and at practices, I hit fungoes, worked on the kids' fielding skills, and operated the Juggs pitching machine (which I bought for the team). When Robert played cornerback for Waldron Academy's football team, I filmed every game. At Merion Mercy Academy, Jennifer excelled at basketball and field hockey—a sport that an urban guy like me had little experience with, but I did what I could to help. It was good times for our family, and for once, it wasn't all about me.

Yeah, it was a retooling period for me and my family, but in hindsight, it was also a retooling period for my career. Carl Mottola moved on in 1972 to become the house drummer at Palumbo's back in South Philly. With his departure, I ended the "dueling drummers" feature that had been one of the highlights of my show for almost a decade. Since it began with Carl, I decided to end it with Carl. The following year, my conductor Rocky Valentine also packed it in. After eight years on the road, he'd also had enough.

A revolving door of drummers followed over the next five years or so. The first of them was a big, tall guy named Roger Ryan who I always thought looked like Lurch from *The Addams Family*. He was a very good drummer and also a virtuoso pothead. Sometimes when he smoked too much, the song tempos would go a little sideways. After one show in Texas at a place called The Loser's Club, Roger's time was all over the place. I was about to give him some shit about it, but was disarmed when he cut me off at the pass and explained that he thought he had just played a great show. He had no idea of how off he was so I told him. "Oh man, I had a great show—sorry you missed it," he replied in a stoner voice that made him sound as if he was in the middle of a Cheech and Chong movie. He really believed he'd just had an outstanding performance. I couldn't help but laugh. You have to appreciate the combination of balls and the smoky, cannabis haze of a statement like that.

Roger was followed by a local jazz drummer named Jimmy Paxson. I not only loved his playing, but also the way he tuned his drums. Those drumheads just popped and had such a presence to them. Unfortunately, he, too, was gone within a year. For a short time, he was replaced by Nick Moffo, the brother of famed opera star Anna Moffo. Next in line was a soon-to-become-famous jazz drummer named Danny Gottlieb. I knew early on that his stint was going to be a short one; the lure of playing straight-ahead jazz was too strong for him to remain content playing "Wild One" and "Volare."

Things stabilized for a while when an extremely gifted drummer named Joe Nero came on board. Joe had graduated as a percussionist from the Curtis Institute in Philadelphia, one of the most elite music conservatories in the world. His inaugural gig with me wasn't exactly on the level of the performances of Mahler, Stravinsky, and Brahms that he was used to at Curtis. I was booked for several weeks at a resort hotel in Bermuda named the Southampton Princess. The hotel's showroom catered to the passengers of the cruise ships that docked nearby, and I was the featured attraction. A small group of native Bermuda musicians led by a gentleman named Gandy Burgess was the house band I'd be working with, but I was told to bring a few extra horn players to augment Gandy's ensemble.

One of them was Roger DeLillo, a very accomplished trombonist who was a member of the studio band for *The Mike Douglas Show*. The other was a saxophonist named Bill Zaccagni, who was recommended for the gig by Palumbo's bandleader, Carmen Dee. Bill was soon to become both a very close friend, and an integral component in the recrafting of my live shows. At six foot four inches, he was an imposing figure who reminded me in many ways of Jackie Gleason. He oozed charisma and talent, had a wicked sense of humor, and filled out a suit just like "The Great One," as Gleason was often called. Every time he walked out of his door, Bill was dressed to the nines in an impressive array of custom-tailored suits and sport coats. He was no less meticulous with his playing. Too bad that quality would be utterly useless on this two-week engagement.

The musicianship in the local band was so poor and irreparable, I couldn't even be mad. All Joe Nero, Bill, Roger, and I could do was laugh. Heavy drinking got us through the shows and extended into our down time. After trying in vain all night to salvage the onstage horn section, Bill and Roger would usually retreat after the shows to the hotel's wine cellar, where they would play armpit fart versions of Thelonius Monk's "Straight No Chaser" and other jazz standards. Bill eventually nicknamed the hotel's house band Gandy Burgess & the Bazooka Band. The offstage drinking got so bad that one day when we were all on the

The gang that tried to save the "Bazooka Band." From left to right: Joe Nero's wife, Pat, Roger DeLillo's wife, Roger, Camille and me, Bill Zaccagni, and Joe Nero.

beach, Roger collapsed in three to four inches of water and was flailing his arms and calling for help, insisting he was drowning. It was just that kind of gig.

Better times were coming. I just didn't know it yet, but I should have. There was no way that all the wholesale changes being implemented in my show wouldn't eventually bring about something good. For starters, I finally replaced the hole in my repertoire that was left when I discontinued the "C Jam Blues" drum duel. I wasn't ready to give up playing the drums just yet, so I began playing a drum feature on the theme from *The David Frost Show*. The tune, called "By George," was composed by master Beatles arranger and producer, George Martin.

It was a bit of a pain in the ass because I had to switch places with the drummer. And I was a lefty, which meant I had to shift the drum set around every time I did the bit. If the audience hadn't dug it so much, I probably would have canned it after a few months. It had its moments though, particularly on a show at the Tamiment Resort in the Poconos. I have no idea what he was doing there, but one of the musicians in the house band that night was famed saxophonist Al Cohn. Al was one of the legendary "Four Brothers" of the Woody Herman big band (Serge Chaloff, Zoot Sims, Stan Getz, and Al), so you can imagine the extra impetus I had to play well that night.

The biggest impact on my show was made by Bill Zaccagni's arrangements. They took me in new directions and brought about a level of musical sophistication that would wow audiences for years to come. After a few warm-up charts on some Barry Manilow tunes, Bill began cranking out one masterpiece after another: a new overture and closer, three killer medleys based on tunes from Stevie Wonder, Bobby Darin, and *Bye Bye Birdie*, and an additional medley of famous saloon songs. Raves from the audiences are one thing, but when jaded, on-stage musicians who have played with just about everybody go out of their way to tell you how great the charts are, you know you've got something special.

The final piece of my rebuilding plan came in April 1978 with the addition of a new drummer named Dave Kovnat. Only in his mid-twenties, Dave came highly recommended by Carl Mottola, who had been teaching him since he was a teenager. Dave's first show with me was a local date in Philadelphia, and it was an uncomfortable night for him. His previous employer, Al Raymond, was a local big band leader. So who do you

On an Australian tour with my new drummer, Dave Kovnat.

think was my back-up band on Dave's inaugural gig with me? You guessed it. Al's eyes shot daggers at him throughout the evening.

Dave's decision to make a career change paid off within a short time. Even though a lot of the work I was doing in the late '70s and early '80s didn't reflect the glamour of my earlier heyday, I still worked at prestigious venues from time to time. We toured Australia together numerous times, played

155

with great big bands like Peter Graves' outfit down in Fort Lauderdale and the Galen Jeter band at the Dallas Playboy Club. I could still draw a full house in Vegas casinos like Caesars and the Desert Inn, and the dozens of wall-to-wall, sold-out shows at South Philly's Palumbo's were borderline historic. They always brought out the best in us. The only person who didn't enjoy them was Camille, who was thrust into the role of social director. She'd get besieged with requests for complimentary tickets from friends and family members.

One of the most memorable engagements during the early '80s was a month-long run at Talk of the Town, London's version of the Copacabana. I really got off on the history of the place. From 1900 through 1957, it was a celebrated music-hall called the London Hippodrome, that hosted the British debut of Tchaikovsky's *Swan Lake.* After it was remodeled and renamed Talk of the Town in 1958, the chic nightclub began featuring headliners like Judy Garland, the Supremes, Frank Sinatra, and Tom Jones.

What turned out to be a really good run at the club was made even better by the visit of a dear friend; Ann-Margret was in town shooting a film, so she and her husband, Roger Smith, stopped by my dressing room. Wearing a tight pink alpaca sweater, Ann looked devastatingly beautiful as always. After briefly catching up with each other about our careers and families, I excused myself for a few minutes to change into my stage clothes, leaving her and Roger with Dave Kovnat. When I came back out, Dave was sitting paralyzed in his chair, sweating profusely. He later told me he had no idea what to say. It hadn't mattered that Roger was there. This wasn't the first time Ann had that type of effect on an overmatched male.

When I had downtime at this point in my life, I was either occupied with family matters or I was on the golf course. Busy with gigs or not, my celebrity status was still very much in effect. Throughout the late '70s and early '80s, I was routinely asked to participate in various fundraising events and golf tournaments.

One of them was for a charity located in the Raleigh-Durham area called *The Duke Children's Classic*, which was sponsored by North Carolina State's head basketball coach, Jim Valvano. I was playing with Perry Como, Frank Sinatra, Dean Martin, Tennessee Ernie Ford, a very young Jay Leno, and several other luminaries.

Perry immediately took a liking to my dad, who I'd brought along for the trip. As we walked along the fairways, the two of them played some Italian geography. Perry—who was Abruzzese and very proud of it—asked my dad what part of Italy his parents came from. Dad stuck out his chest and proudly proclaimed, "Marché." Perry looked at him, shook his head side to side and said in a sarcastic, condescending tone, "You're no Italian." Dad looked like he'd been sucker-punched by Sonny Liston. He was totally deflated. Perry picked up on his distress and immediately started laughing and gave him a hug. My dad didn't golf that well, but he definitely won the tournament's Most Gullible Italian Award by a landslide.

Shortly after the Duke Children's Classic, I traveled to Tampa for another golf benefit whose celebrity lineup included Dodgers' manager Tommy Lasorda and New York Yankee legend Joe DiMaggio. The tournament director told me Tommy wanted to meet me. We hit it off right away. Tommy put his arm around me and said, "I knew as soon as you opened your mouth that you were Abruzzese like me." I didn't want to go through the whole Marché thing again like my dad had gone through with Perry Como, so I just agreed with him. It was only a half lie; my mom's side of the family was Abruzzese.

Tommy was a street guy like me, but Joe "D" was baseball royalty. It wasn't going to be as simple as my one-on-one meeting with Tommy. I had to be pre-screened by his handler, a very nice man named Carl. He was brief and to the point: certain topics of discussion (namely, Sinatra and Marilyn Monroe) were off limits, and if I wanted an autograph, Joe would be happy to sign a baseball for me. Joe was somewhat quiet, but a beautiful cat nevertheless. And you better believe I still have that ball.

Most likely, you've noticed by now that I haven't talked very much about my mom. Tough subject—a *real* tough subject. I have to admit I'm jealous of celebrities like Don Rickles and Tiger Woods, who frequently and affectionately praise their parents and credit them for their success. My dad would definitely fit that description: I'd be nothing without him; he meant the world to me. My mom? Not by a long shot.

I'd known ever since I was young that something was not quite right with her. Maybe it first dawned on me when she once picked me up and flung me across the room. The bed luckily broke my fall, but that was merely a coincidence. It hadn't been part of her initial game plan. The offense I committed that had set her off faded from my memory decades ago. But how bad could it have been? I was only three or four.

You could refer to my Mom as high-strung, bipolar, schizophrenic, manic depressive—anything you want, but no categorizing can adequately explain how she could go from a nurturing, loving mother one moment, and in the blink of an eye, be transformed into an incoherent, enraged Mommy Dearest.

I grew up with the ever-present threat that if I came home fifteen minutes late from hanging with my friends, I'd get slapped around. While other kids stayed up until 10:00 p.m., I always had to leave early to avoid hearing her screaming my name from two blocks away. And then there were the all too common occurrences of the projectiles that were thrown at me for some perceived misdeed. Whatever was handy would do the trick: a potato, an apple, a kitchen utensil, whatever was within arms' reach when she had a head of steam on.

In all fairness, I'd be a total wimp to even mention any of this if that's all there was. This was South Philly in the '40s and '50s; an Italian mother who was tough on her kid was not exactly front-page news. The real action with Mom took place once my recording career took off in 1959. From the moment "Kissin' Time" hit, my life in show biz became the center of

My mom in 1969.

Mom's universe. As the hits kept coming, the woman who could have cared less about my musical and comedic pursuits for the first seventeen years of my life became consumed with every phase of my career.

It went way past stereotypical stage-parent behavior and went right into textbook obsessive-compulsive disorder territory. She knew absolutely nothing about show biz, but nevertheless felt she could make the calls on the songs I sung, my on-stage banter, the clothes I wore when I performed, and every other aspect of my act. She loved feeling important. I'd say to her, "Who the hell do you think you are? Lynne Duddy and Jerry Bressler?" (two of the more prominent producers who staged nightclub acts in the '60s and '70s). That shut her up temporarily, but she would soon jump back into action.

To Mom, I was the moon, the sun, and the stars—the absolute center of the universe. As disturbing as that was, I could have dealt with it. The larger problem was, she wanted everyone else to feel that way too, and couldn't understand when they didn't. When Joe Nero first came over to my house to discuss the possibility of drumming on the road with me, my mother pulled him aside and gave him the lay of the land—working conditions, stage attire, salary, and other pertinent info about the job. When an uncomfortable silence set in, she picked something up from Joe's body language that implied one or more aspects of her sales pitch didn't sit well with him. She quickly addressed his temporary lack of reverence and awe over the possibility of working with me by letting him know, "But you know, Joe, you get to eat with Bobby when you're on the road." How demented an outlook—like the whole world should be as obsessed with me as much as she was.

Titanic fights were commonplace rituals between Mom and me, and also between her and Frankie Day. Issues as trivial as the color of my tie during a particular show would be enough to set her off. These lectures and rants could take place anywhere: while I was in the bathroom, over the phone, in the car on the way to a show, or as soon as I came off the stage. Palumbo's shows were the worst because all her friends were there. As predictable as Old Faithful, she'd harangue me more than usual, believing that her suggestions would ensure everyone would be thoroughly impressed.

Mom saved her worst moments for the dinner table. Evening meals at my house often descended into bloody, savage battlegrounds where, unfortunately, I wasn't the only target. She couldn't exist in an atmosphere of love and serenity, and usually viewed such situations as a vacuum that needed to be filled with assorted displays of venom. If she couldn't ruin a beautiful dinner by criticizing something Camille had cooked, she would take the easier path and go after low hanging fruit. "You know you never loved your grandmother," she would say to me out of nowhere, and like an idiot, I would take the bait and go nuts.

Going after me or my wife was one thing—Camille usually just humored her to keep the peace—but every time my kids became her targets, our home life reached all-time lows. One night, we had a special dinner to celebrate a singing and acting role Jennifer had successfully performed in *Oliver!*, her school play. "I was just like Dad," she gushed with pride as we drank a toast to her. I couldn't have been happier for her, but not my mom. "Don't you ever compare yourself to your father," she hissed at her granddaughter. "He was already a star making a living at your age. You'll *never* be like him." You can only imagine the fight that followed as I agonizingly witnessed my daughter melt down in front of me and then run out of the room drenched in tears.

You'd have thought my mother had been adopted because she was so completely different from her mother. Grandma Lena was a kind and loving woman, and as I've previously noted, a world-class cook. Her daughter picked up none of those traits, *especially* the cooking part. Mom couldn't have boiled spaghetti if she wanted to—which she never did. She preferred to have other people wait on her. And even when she had an occasional moment during which she showed a little warmth and affection, you knew her alter-ego "Jennie" was always lurking close by. For almost three decades, my grandmother had tried her best to intervene between my mother and me, but after she passed away in the early '70s, that emotional shield was gone.

To the people who knew my mother as the stylish, upbeat and eternally happy Jennie who attended most of my Philadelphia and South Jersey shows, all these revelations must come as a shock. But, of course she was happy! This is what she lived for: the reflected glory of being the mother of an international teen idol. If I'm on stage being adored by thousands of fans, it meant *she* was being adored. A very disturbing, one-way bond connected Mom to me. If it were a cocktail drink, it would be one part *Psycho* combined with a twist of *I am he, as you are he, as you are me, and we are all together.* It couldn't have been more obvious: Mom was living her life through me.

At this point, the 800-pound gorilla in the room is punching me in the head demanding some attention: Why did I allow all of this to happen? Why didn't I stand up to her? In my early twenties, I chalked it up to immaturity and my traditional Italian upbringing. Parents were god-like figures to be feared and respected. I'd grown up watching my mom and dad live with my grandparents. We always lived together. That's the way things were done in our family, and that's the reason why I originally moved my parents and grandparents in with me back in 1963.

BOBBY RYDELL'S

"Am I Losing My Son?"

That was her son up there, singing under the big white light, clapping his hands and swinging his body in time to his song. Jenny Ridarelli looked around at the rest of the audience. *Kids,* she thought, *and night-clubbing already.*

She turned to her husband. "Look at this, Al, a house full of teenagers. When we were their age, did we go to night clubs?"

"Jenny, look, there are lots of adults in the room. Besides, it's prom season. And they like Bobby Rydell. Anyway, so they're kids, so what? Where would he be without them?"

Where would he be . . . ? she thought. *In some audience now, watching some 19-year-old singer? Would he have a date of his own and time of his own to do the things most kids his age do? Would he have* (*Continued on page* 55)

By MICKI SIEGEL

42

164

MOTHER ASKS:

This clipping from an old teen magazine may have withered and turned yellow with age, but its content is still terrifying to me.

It was the worst decision I ever made. My grandparents were no problem; they were always a pleasure to be with—not to mention the bonus of having incredible meals served on a daily basis. Mom was another story altogether. Within days, she began berating me saying, "What'd you do to me?" There were no trolley cars right outside our front door (like on 11th Street) that could take her back and forth to her daily ritual of shopping in center city Philadelphia. That part of her life had come to a grinding halt. Little by little, my father was reduced from being Mom's husband to being her chauffeur. Like my grandmother, he too tried to shield me from her as much as he could, but I could tell he was resigned to his fate.

After enduring almost a decade of living under the same roof with my mother, I finally woke up and recognized the disastrous effect it was having on me and my family. In the early '70s, I resolved to get Mom out of the house. After a few weeks of making the rounds with a local real estate agent, I bought my parents their own home. It was only a few blocks away, but to my mother, it might as well have been on Jupiter.

My parents never moved in. Mom couldn't take not being on top of me, constantly controlling every aspect of my life and career. She sold the house I bought for her and kept the money. From that point on, you could explain away my inability to stand up to her and kick her out—or at least shelter my family from her madness—as inertia, guilt, weakness, or all of the above. Whatever the reason, my parents would continue to live with me for the remainder of their lives.

🎼 VERSE 3

The retooling I went through in the early-to-mid-'70s was not just limited to my musicians, my act, and my family life. Frankie Day had been my close friend and mentor for almost a decade and a half. We'd logged hundreds of thousands of miles together, celebrated a healthy dose of triumphs, and weathered the few defeats we'd encountered along the way, but now we were nearing the end of our road.

I can only remember one major argument with him in all that time, and it occurred on one of my early Australian tours. I was doing my imitations schtick and the audience wasn't responding. From offstage, Frankie motioned to me to keep going, but I switched over to the drum thing with Carl. In my dressing room after the show, Frankie jumped in my face yelling, "When I tell you to do something, just do it!" I told him to go fuck himself and almost as soon as the words came out of my mouth, the situation turned into a one-and-done spat that was quickly forgotten.

In contrast, our eventual split was something that grew slowly over time. Frankie had moved out to California in the early '70s, gotten married, and then relocated to Hawaii. That was the start of a long-distance relationship that was workable up until the filming of *That Lady from Peking*. I wanted Frankie to come to Australia with me, but between his new wife and his house in paradise, he'd gotten too comfortable. He didn't want to come. If I was in his circumstances, I don't know if I would have wanted to leave home either, but at the time, it really pissed me off. I was out there all by myself and the film looked like it was going to be a bomb. I had no one to speak up for my interests.

Frankie had done a marvelous job guiding my recording, concert, and TV careers, but he generally fell short in the movie department. He just didn't have a basic feel for the film market, which led him to continually overplay his hand. Knowing what to ask for was a major problem for him. Frankie did a great job landing me the *Bye Bye Birdie* role, but settled for a buyout—a flat $25,000 fee—instead of taking a lesser figure plus back-end points. When the film became a smash, not having a share of the profits really cost me. Similarly, he blew a major role for me in another film version of a hit Broadway show by asking for too much. I was up for a role in Columbia Pictures' *Oliver!*, but it never happened because Frankie's business negotiations were so ham-handed. That film went on to rack up eleven Academy Awards nominations, winning six of them.

Still, the good Frankie had done for my career far outweighed the bad. Our artist-management relationship had started in 1957 without a contract between us—just a simple warm handshake. It ended the same way in 1974. I'll always feel indebted to him for the career he built for me.

After Frankie and I went our separate paths, I navigated my show biz affairs for five or six years by myself. Lee Solomon, my agent at the William Morris Agency, was feeding me enough gigs to keep my name in circulation. Then in 1976, I was aided by the municipal referendum that brought gambling to Atlantic City. Two years later in the spring of 1978, Resorts Casino Hotel opened and was quickly followed by Caesars and the Tropicana in '79, the Golden Nugget and the Sands in '80, and Ballys, the Playboy, and the Claridge in '81. With all these new showrooms opening up virtually in my backyard, I felt like a fox who had broken into the henhouse.

Two of the first engagements I had in casino-revamped Atlantic City happened at Resorts shortly after it opened. In both, I was an opening act, but I didn't mind; I was working with some comedic legends. The first was with Buddy Hackett, who was one part genius and three parts lunatic. On the opening night of a three-day run, I walked into his dressing room just before I hit the stage and it was ice cold. He had the air conditioner blasting and he was sitting there butt naked with a towel across his lap. Buddy wished me well, and then I walked out and did my act. It was a great set and I left the stage to a thunderous ovation. When Buddy took over, logic, sanity, and the laws of the physical universe no longer applied. His opening monologue went something like this:

> *"You liked that guy? Not me. I didn't want him as an opening act. I told Resorts that I wanted someone else. But then I get a call from some guy named Nunzio. I told him the same thing; I wanted a different opening act. He tried to convince me that Bobby would work out great, but I wouldn't budge. I stood my ground.*
>
> *Back in my hotel room I had a prized pet clam that I was very attached to. The morning after Nunzio had talked to me, I woke up and found a severed clams head at the bottom of my bed."*

Pretty twisted stuff, huh? But the audience ate it up and howled with laughter. The next headliner I opened for hadn't built his career and reputation by demonstrating a high degree of mental balance either. But man, what a sharp dresser! Nobody could wear a tuxedo like Jerry Lewis. There were some quirks attached though. Jerry always wears brand-new, snow-white sweat socks and black penny loafers (even with a tux) and he never uses a pair of underwear more than once. Don't ask me how I know, but they wind up in the trash after a single usage. I also learned he's a world-class practical joker. Every time I turned my head during our three-day run together, Jerry would sneak into my dressing room to steal or hide my bowties and handkerchiefs minutes before I had to hit the stage.

But he also had a very serious side and an impeccable eye for

The electronic marquee at Resorts Casino Hotel in Atlantic City.

staging. Watching my rehearsal before our opening night, Jerry stopped me in mid-song and shouted out in a very authoritative voice, "Stop! Hold It! Bobby! Your conductor is standing in your light. The audience will be watching him instead of you." I looked at what he was talking about and realized he was one hundred percent correct. The audience's sightline was instantly improved once we made the correction. The man was a perfectionist who knew his stuff.

I was staying busy enough, but didn't love running my own affairs, so I eventually gave having a manager another shot. In the late '70s, a guy named Stan Seidenberg began handling my career. He did a decent job, but in 1985 he more than earned his money. Stan hooked me up with Dick Fox, an ex-William Morris agent who had a history of putting together a number of successful doo-wop shows. Dick had a concept for a new show he wanted me to consider.

Golden Boys in training (Me, Fabian, and Frankie): Dick Fox was originally calling us "Philadelphia's Royalty of Rock".

His idea was to combine three South Philly teen idols in a stage revue that would be called *Philadelphia's Royalty of Rock.* The three names he'd settled on were Frankie Avalon, Fabian, and me. (It wasn't that hard a decision. There was only one other teen idol from South Philly: James Darren.) Dick had already secured the Premier Theater in suburban Detroit for our first show, including two days of rehearsal at the venue to put it all together. The basic schematic was an extension of Frankie Avalon's stage show. We opened with an instrumental overture of "The Way We Were," followed by an edited, video presentation of vintage film footage from all our careers. The three of us finally hit the stage together singing "Bandstand Boogie," Dick Clark's signature theme song.

The show then broke down into solo segments in which we each did our individual hits and then rejoined to sing the Righteous Brothers' "Rock and Roll Heaven." That was the lead-in to the show's tribute segment. I sang Bobby Darin's "Mack the Knife," Fabian did his Elvis thing with "Hard Headed Woman," and Frankie took on the role of Ricky Nelson with "Hello Mary Lou." A reprieve of "Rock and Roll Heaven" closed it out, followed by the three of us singing "Old Time Rock and Roll," and then Frankie's patented Mickey Mouse theme finished off the show.

Got all that? I laid it out in two paragraphs. Now why don't you go and try to put all those moving parts together in two days. It ain't so easy. Any time you put three stars accustomed to a lifetime of pampering on the same bill, you're asking for agita (Italian for heartburn). There were debates and arguments over a laundry list of issues. A big one for me was the order in which we appeared. I was supposed to open, Fabian was second, and Frankie was the closer. Part of it was the usual ego-itis. Just like all athletes want to be starters, every singer wants to headline.

But my main gripe was based on something more important: I hated the Mickey Mouse theme ending. I didn't want to be up there looking like an idiot, singing, *"Now it's time to say goodbye to all our company, M-I-C-K-E-Y, M-O-U-S-E."* I hated it. I was embarrassed by it. I wanted to pick a different ending—almost any ending but that one.

Frank pulled me aside and said, "Bob, please. Give it a chance. I'm telling you—I've been doing it for years and it

An early Golden Boys show.

goes over like gangbusters. Just try it." Two hours after the first show kicked off, I had to swallow my pride and apologize to Frank, but I really didn't mind having to eat crow on this one. The house went berserk when we sang it. The Mickey Mouse bit wasn't the only thing that was a hit; the entire show was a smash. We'd been part of an electrified, history-making evening. The future looked bright and limitless . . . except for that name . . . and those other two guys I had to be around all the time. We'd be sailing some rough seas for a while.

Over time, the name thing was worked out with minimal problems. After two or three shows, *Philadelphia's Royalty of Rock* was changed to *Dick Fox's Golden Boys of Bandstand,* and then eventually shortened to *Dick Fox's Golden Boys.* Other kinks in the show were worked out and adjusted as

Taking a bow after my solo spot in the show.

we went along until everyone was comfortable. Dick was at every gig during the early days of the show, steering the ship and making sure it stayed on course. The three of us Golden Boys being up each others' asses all the time would take a little more work.

We were all good friends, especially Frank and me, since we'd been playing with each other since he was thirteen and I was ten. As for Fabian, I couldn't count the number of oldies shows I'd done with him. But we'd all existed as solo acts for most of our careers. Whenever we were on a bill with other people, we always quickly returned to our solo tours. It was like getting married all over again and having to adjust to your new partner's habits, likes, and dislikes. Actually, it was worse: It was like being married to two wives and having to adjust to *both* of their habits, likes, and dislikes.

Fabian was easy; he gets along with everybody. Frank and I had a much older and closer relationship, but it was a far more complex one. Problems started early on.

When the Golden Boys were on the road in Cleveland, we went out to eat at what turned out to be a really lousy Italian restaurant. I could barely get my food down, but Frank was really doing a number on some pizza. "This food sucks," I said in disgust. "How can you eat this shit?" Frank ignored me and continued wolfing down the slice he'd been working on. And then I delivered the fateful words: "You ain't a real Italian." For the next three gigs, I got the silent treatment. Frank held a grudge. I tried to initiate conversations with him, but all I'd get would be one word answers, or no answer at all. I'd say, "How you doin' Cheech?" "Fine," or "OK," would be his typical reply, and then he'd walk away.

It all came to a head one day after a show. He was combing his hair in the dressing room. I said to him, "That was a really good show, wasn't it?" and got no response. Finally, I broke the ice and asked, "What? Are you still pissed at me? We have a hell of a lot more dates to do this summer, and if you're not gonna talk to me, it'll be one very long tour." Frank let me have it with both barrels and finished up saying, "I'll talk to you, but I'm never eating with you ever again." Two hours later, we had dinner. It was like nothing ever happened.

Both of us knew a winner when we saw it. We weren't about to wreck the opportunity this new Golden Boys extravaganza presented us because of an insult over a lousy slice of pizza. Besides, I had some other challenges that were complicating

Frankie and me having "a talk" in the dressing room while Fabian looks on.

my life. One was small; the other would take three decades to work out.

The small one was fixed in a day. Stan Seidenberg was out. In 1986, I performed at a benefit concert in Scranton, Pennsylvania for a close friend, a priest named Father Joseph Sica. I didn't like the way Stan had handled the finances and we had a falling out. When I fell, it was right into the arms of Dick Fox, who has been my manager for the last thirty years. If only he knew back then what he was getting into.

From the moment I traded in my teen idol uniform and took on the role of a tuxedoed saloon singer, I was on the clock: *"So make it one for my baby, and one more for the road."* You know what I mean. Drinking comes with the cultural territory of working casino showrooms; the romance of the bottle was staring me right in the face. The songs I sang celebrated that culture, and most of my musical heroes lived that life: Frank Sinatra, Sammy Davis Jr., Dean Martin—they all had that indelible image of '60s cool: a cigarette in one hand and a shot glass in the other.

In my younger years, drinking was a minor recreational pastime. Sure, I might have tied one on from time to time, but until I passed fifty, I was never really a problem drinker. My first taste of alcohol was a beer when I was thirteen years old. I was at a party with some other kids. A few years later, my Dad advised me, "When you get old enough to drink alcohol, don't

My glasses of liquor weren't really that big; the increasing number and frequency of normal-sized glasses was the problem. This shot was taken years later at my 60th birthday party.

drink whiskey; it'll knock you out. Drink scotch." Eventually, I took him up on it. Around the time I hit my '30s, I'd settled into a modest routine of drinking a glass of Dewars scotch and water before dinner and maybe a Galliano with ice afterwards. Ten years later, my drink of choice had become a Beefeater gin martini and my overall appetite for alcohol had grown, but I was still firmly in control of the horizontal and the vertical.

That all changed one day in 1992 when Camille came home and said, "Bobby, sit down. I have to tell you something." Then she paused for a moment, looked at me with an awkward, but loving smile and said, "I have breast cancer." Just like that. No beating around the bush. A routine mammogram at nearby Lankenau Hospital had revealed a tumor.

Within days, Camille underwent a lumpectomy and a torturous round of radiation and chemotherapy. Miraculously she beat whatever was going on in her body and was soon in remission. She was doing fine; I wasn't. From that moment on, I lived in constant fear that her cancer would return. My initial solution was as simple and direct as the way my wife told me she was ill: I was going to anesthetize myself (now with vodka) as often as needed. I just wanted to be happy again and end my emotional pain.

I began drinking heavily, particularly after my shows. Oh, I was quite functional for the most part. The drinking dulled my anxiety about Camille's state of health, and I have to admit, I was enjoying my new alcohol-fueled lifestyle. When I was high, I was good-time Charlie. I was rarely a belligerent drinker who gets bombed or becomes argumentative and then instigates a fistfight with someone. It all would have been the perfect set-up if not for the physical toll it was taking on me. I knew it, and so did Camille.

She decided to do something about it in the summer of '92. It had been a busy winter and spring with the Golden Boys, and when summer rolled around, I had the good fortune of being reunited with my old friend Dick Clark. I'd been booked through Labor Day to star in *American Bandstand: A Musical Happening*, a large-scale production show at the Tropicana Casino in Atlantic City. The showroom was packed every night.

The Tropicana's marquee advertising "American Bandstand: A Musical Happening."

I couldn't have asked for a better situation professionally, but I was well aware of the always-present temptations of the casino environment.

I was friends with a lot of the local guys in the band. Sometimes, I'd have a taste with them before we went on stage, but after the show, drinking was a nightly affair. Once the curtain closed, I could be found in one of the Trop's lounges or on the casino floor tying one on. Camille would try to get me to come back to our hotel room, or sometimes she'd get pissed off, pack her bags and leave the Trop for our house in Longport, New Jersey. The morning after every one of these bouts, I'd apologize over and over and promise it wouldn't happen again. Then a few days later we'd repeat the same dance. I was like a turntable needle stuck on a groove of a broken record that doomed it to infinite repetitions. In spite of everything, Camille was always there by my side. This was

One of my solo gigs in front of a large, outdoors audience.

the new life I'd chosen for myself. Only she was smart enough to recognize that it was taking me down a bad road.

Luckily for me, it was a relatively lengthy road. In spite of what I was doing, I didn't consider myself to be a drunk. Whether I was right or wrong with that self-assessment didn't matter much to me. The way I saw it, I was still doing a good job of holding my own, and I'd remain that way for quite a while. Dick Fox kept rolling the dice with the Golden Boys, my solo career was as busy as I wanted it to be, my bills were getting paid, and my family's comfortable lifestyle continued on without skipping a beat.

I still had enough on the ball to navigate past my inner demons and be a good Italian parent. One day I decided I needed to instill some ethnic pride in my children. Robert was no problem; he readily identified himself as a South Philly Italian. He even told people that's where he came from, despite having lived his entire life in the suburbs. When he finally got married, you can guess where he immediately moved to when he began raising his family. Jennifer wasn't quite so obliging. After watching her date a parade of young men with last names like Smith, Schwartz, and O'Sullivan, but none that ended with a good solid vowel, I asked her why she never dated Italians. "I'm not going out with any Guidos," I was told. Jeez, if I wanted that kind of abuse, I could have re-enlisted at Fort Dix for another round of basic training or picked another dumb argument with Cheech.

The road continued on for me, but not for someone who had played a huge role in my career. The death of Cameo-Parkway founder Bernie Lowe in 1993 should have closed a symbolic door on my teen idol era. Instead, I spent the next two years working on preserving its legacy. In the summer of '93, I recorded *The Bobby Rydell Story* at Sigma Sound Studios. An infomercial company called Regal Entertainment wanted to release a collection of my old records, but Allen Klein—whose ABKCO Entertainment owned the rights to all that material—wanted a gazillion dollars for the licensing rights. I immediately said the hell with that and called up Allan Slutsky, who I'd befriended the summer before when he played guitar in the Michael Pedicin Orchestra, the Tropicana's house band. I asked him if he could transcribe and reproduce my original hits and make them sound just like they did in the early '60s. Allan threw the challenge right back at me and said, "I can if you can still sing the way you did back in the '60s."

We got remarkably close. I was pleasantly surprised to find I could still sing a lot of my old hits in their original keys, and still pull off songs like "The Cha-Cha-Cha" and "I've Got Bonnie" that I hadn't performed in years. It was nice to know that even though I was aging everywhere else in my body, my vocal chords were still young. Two years later in 1995, the original, recorded hit versions came out on a K-Tel album titled *The Best of Bobby Rydell*. Allen Klein must have dropped his asking price from a gazillion dollars to $25,000. Welcome to the music business.

A series of pleasant surprises greeted me in 1995. Hands down, the best news of all involved Camille; she was in full remission and feeling much better. In fact, she was feeling well enough to accompany me on a trip to Hawaii, where I was headlining a concert that reunited me with my old friend and mentor Frankie Day. Shortly after returning home, I found out that Paul McCartney had mentioned me in the *Beatles Anthology* CD collection and credited one of my records as the basis for the "Yeah, Yeahs" in "She Loves You." (He probably got the idea from the background vocals in "We Got Love.") It was nice to know that thirty-two years after we last met, Paul (now Sir Paul) still remembered me.

Outside of my wife's recovery, my favorite other 1995 event came on October 15th. After years of steady campaigning by my lifelong fan club President Linda Ferrino (Hoffman)—the city of Philadelphia renamed the 2400 to 2500 block of 11th

*Linda Ferrino (Hoffman)—my steadfast friend and fan club president
—at the dedication ceremony for Bobby Rydell Boulevard.*

Street in South Philadelphia, *Bobby Rydell Boulevard.* The new street sign was placed at the corner of 11th and Moyamensing. Philadelphia had previously honored me in 1987 by inducting me—along with John Coltrane, Dizzy Gillespie, Bessie Smith, Bill Haley, Chubby Checker, Leopold Stokowski, and others—on the Broad Street Walk of Fame with a bronze plaque. It was a thrill, but this time around, they threw one helluva party into the mix: close to a thousand people in the street, a parade led by the Mummers with a trolley car carrying all my friends and family, and me and my daughter and grandson, Robert, bringing up the rear sitting atop a '50s pink Cadillac. I was extremely grateful and humbled by the experience.

The renamed street sign.

*Addressing a huge crowd of family, friends, and fans on a street
corner where I used to hang out and spin 45s.*

The biblical quote I learned in Catholic school that a prophet
cannot be honored in his home country seemed to not apply to
me, at least not in South Philly. But I wasn't much of a prophet.
With all the positive things that were happening in my life,
you'd figure I would have taken my foot off the gas pedal for
awhile and enjoyed the ride, or at least cut back on the things
that were keeping my life in a state of turmoil. Maybe if I'd
stayed at home, that might have worked out. Unfortunately,
the usual temptations of the road had other plans for me.

The Golden Boys were in Biloxi, Mississippi, and we had a
free day after our performance there. Frank took off in a limo
to go to New Orleans, which was only a ninety-minute car ride

away. When he came back that night, I could tell he'd been drinking and was in a foul mood. He started giving Fabian a hard time. Fabe wisely just walked away, so Frank switched targets and started in on me. "You know Bob, you should get rid of the *Birdie* medley. It's not doing anything for your act," he said in a snooty tone. I had him matched glass-for-glass and point-for-point that night, and I was in just as nasty a mood. I told him I'd think about it, and then countered, "Frank, y'know that tune you do—'The Good Guys?' It stinks. You should take it out of your act."

"Take it out?" he said defensively, obviously finding it hard to believe I could say that about a tune that he considered an essential part of his act. Eventually we both backed off and retreated to the downstairs lounge for a few more drinks. Frank started messing around, giving me some soft love taps across my cheek and I gave him a few back. Nothing serious, but then he nails me with a hard one so I give him a good shot to the jaw and cut his lip. All of a sudden, we're going at it like two wrestlers in a cage match. Security had to break up the fight. Once things calmed down, the guards escorted each of us back to our hotel rooms.

The next morning we had an early morning lobby call for a flight to Long Island, New York. We were supposed to play the Westbury Music Fair that evening. I woke up in a pool of blood. A half-hour later, I saw Frank in the lobby. We both looked at each other's bruised faces and almost simultaneously said, "What the fuck did we do last night?" That evening, we took the stage with swollen faces and black eyes, and, for obvious reasons, omitted the punch-drunk fighter, comedy routine that we sometimes did.

The cuts, bumps, and bruises healed: a few ice packs, some hydrogen peroxide, and a few Band-Aids was all it took. What was going on inside my head and my soul was not quite so easily mended. As the new millennium approached, it was apparent to everyone but me that this was my new life: play some golf, drink, hang out with friends and family, do a few gigs, sometimes drink to the point where I became an asshole, watch the Phillies and Eagles, listen to Sinatra and some of my favorite big band drummers, drink, do a Golden Boys tour, and then drink again.

It was all so haphazard. When was I going to take stock of what I was doing? Where was the self-analysis? In hindsight almost two decades later, I can throw out lots of reasons for my self-destructive behavior: My mother? I don't like that one. Yeah, she was no gem, but I had decades to move her out of the house and have clear sailing for Camille and myself. As you know by now, I didn't do it, so I'm not entitled to that excuse. And besides, as bad as she was, the sheer goodness and decency of my dad offset a lot of the harm she did. Camille and the cancer? Maybe the first few years were understandable, but she was doing great and had been in remission for almost seven years. A genetic disposition to addictive behavior? Listen, I'm old school. I don't want to let myself off the hook with some bullshit, modern terminology where every aspect of bad conduct can be explained away with some psychological label. I simply had no answers for the way I was living my life, and

I didn't want them anyway. Translation: I was going to stay on the same dumb path.

Sometime in the late '90s, Cheech and I had a booking as a duo at the Orleans Hotel and Casino in Las Vegas. I was drinking before the show, which was not that unusual. What *was* different that night was I didn't know when to stop. How I got through my part of the act I can't tell you. Instead of singing my usual repertoire, I broke rank and called out an old standard off the top of my head. I might have called "Night and Day," "All the Things You Are," or "All of Me." But if it had been James Brown's "Mother Popcorn," I wouldn't have known the difference. I remember leaning against the piano and singing something, but from the backstage, post-show reaction, it must have been bad.

"I'll never work with that fuckin' drunk again," Frank fumed to Dave Kovnat. It was more a sign of frustration than a real threat. He was just worried about me. Once he calmed down, Frank was lamenting to anyone within earshot in the dressing room area: "What the hell's he doing to himself? He's ruining his career."

Something was going to give at some point and eventually, it did. A two-year period that began in December 2000 turned out to be my personal Waterloo. My dad—my lifelong buddy and inspiration—had been courageously fighting prostate cancer and diabetes for several years, but he was finally running out of gas.

My dad's decline reminded me of another inspirational figure of mine whose last years were also painful to witness. I saw

Sinatra perform at the Sands in Atlantic City a few years before his 1998 death. Frank was singing his "Come Fly With Me" opener and, in spite of having large teleprompters in front of him, he was still forgetting the lyrics. It was sad, yet I saw a brief flash of his former brilliance when he absolutely killed it on "One For My Baby." His voice may have been gone, but he could still really tell a story. I knew that night that he was near the end. The day Sinatra could no longer spin his musical tales, would be his last.

My dad expressed himself in a far more humble way than Sinatra. From the time he was in his teens, he loved to drive. He spent his life driving everywhere, with me, his wife, friends, and family members. It was his way of telling people that he loved them. Near the end he told me," When it comes time where I can't drive a car, put me in my coffin." Several days later, he couldn't drive the car anymore. On December 14th at the age of eighty-five, he passed away.

I didn't have very long to mourn for him. Camille had been in remission for nine years, but shortly after the New Year, her doctors discovered that the cancer had returned and metasta-sized to her liver, her lungs, and finally . . . everywhere. I was a basket case. When my old friend and co-mentor Kal Mann died in 2001, I barely noticed. Between my dad's passing and my worries about Camille, I ran out of tears to shed.

A brief moment of comfort came when Ann-Margret visited my home. After all the years, I still called her Kim and she'd call me Hugo, or occasionally, "Mr. Ridarelli." As quaint as it may seem, it was just what I needed. She knew what I was

Me and my dad in his last year.

going through and wanted to offer some support. At the time, Camille was rapidly losing her hair so Ann showed her how to wrap a scarf turban-style around her head so she wouldn't be self-conscious when she went out in public.

Jimmy Darren would also call from time to time to try and lighten the mood. Always a practical joker, he'd call the house, and if Camille answered, he'd disguise his voice and say something threatening like, "Hey, this is Vinny. Bobby's got my drums and I want 'em back!" Camille would get all flustered until she finally realized it was just Jimmy playing her like a fiddle. Throughout my life, I've been blessed to have friends like Ann and Jimmy, who have looked out for me and helped me get through tough times.

Too often, my mother wasn't one of them. Despite what Camille and I were going through, she cut no slack to anyone. It was all one big inconvenience to her. First she lost my Dad (one chauffeur down) and now Camille had become too ill to drive (two chauffeurs down). She was stranded in the house unless I drove her somewhere or she called a cab. On a particularly tough day when my mother was giving her a hard time, my wife uncharacteristically fought back, telling her, "Mom, I have stage four cancer. There is no stage five!" My mother backed off, but only momentarily. There were no extenuating circumstances that would bring about a change in her behavior. She was going to do what she'd always done.

But I was changing dramatically, and predictably, not for the good. Still living in the naive mindset of a teen idol where death was something that happened to other people, the mere thought of having to live my life without Camille was inconceivable to me. The fear that I'd lived with for nine years, since Camille was first diagnosed, had now escalated to a much stronger emotion: sheer terror.

It came in the form of a double-edged threat. In my fifty years on this planet, I'd never loved any other woman; I couldn't bear the thought of losing her. But in all those same years, I'd also never done too many things for myself other than pursue my career. When it came to all the boring, day-to-day issues that most people deal with, I was a complete virgin. Paying bills, making doctor's appointments, balancing a checkbook, scheduling my life? All of those things had always been handled by someone else: in my childhood by my parents; in my teens and twenties by my manager; and throughout the rest of my life, by Camille.

Outwardly, I was supportive and loving to my wife as she courageously fought the good fight. But I was still doing things that hurt her deeply. She knew I was still drinking, but had no idea how high I'd up'd the ante. I kept inventing lower and lower levels of rock bottom, if that was possible. Out on the road, Dave walked in on me one day in my hotel room and was stunned to find me in a drunken stupor saying the Rosary as if it were a mantra. "Bob, what the hell are you doing?" he said in an exasperated tone and walked out shaking his head in disbelief.

I'd run out of places to turn to. The bottle wasn't working; prayer wasn't working; and no matter what I did or whatever deals I tried to cut in private with God, Camille's condition continued to deteriorate. I don't know how, but she never lost her sense of humor; it was her way of coping. "It figures I'm the only person who goes through chemo and doesn't lose any weight," she joked to me one day.

She was struggling mightily to hang on until the birth of her fourth grandchild. Jennifer had married and was eight months pregnant with her first child. At least that prayer was answered. Camille got to hold a beautiful, healthy baby boy named Caden Dulin.

In the final stages in September 2003, I spent virtually all of my time at her bedside at Lankenau Hospital. I was determined

Me and Camille with our grandsons, Robert and Tristen.

to blow off a three-day gig in Vegas, but Camille insisted I go. She wanted to get me the hell out of her hospital room. I wasn't doing her any good camped out crying, looking like she'd already died. Reluctantly, I hopped on a plane and did the first two nights, but then my son called to tell me she'd taken a major turn for the worse. I bagged the third night in Vegas and got back one day before Camille passed.

Arriving back at the hospital just after midnight, I walked into her room and found everyone in our immediate family there. She made it to the morning of September 15th, and then we finally decided to end the desperate measures and let her go peacefully. Fifteen minutes after the doctors took her off life support, the monitors flatlined. My wife of thirty-five years was gone.

CHORUS 3

left the hospital in complete despair, with no idea how I was going to get past the next hour, let alone the rest of my life. Within a short time, the answer came to me; it was the usual bad one. I spent six days between Camille's passing and her funeral in my bedroom drinking vodka and crying. Somehow I was able to get straight in time for the funeral. My good friend Father Sica cut through the sorrow by delivering a perfect eulogy that reminded us all how lucky we had been to have Camille in our lives. Sitting in a packed St. Margaret's Church with hundreds of people who loved Camille and me also helped, but it was only a quick fix. Once I was home, everyone and everything disappeared into a liquid void over ice.

My mother felt bad for me and the kids, but didn't seem to be grieving all that much. I'd see her in the morning and then wouldn't have to deal with her for the rest of the day. Living alone with Mom would have been an agonizing experience, but I was saved by her obsession with shopping and converting every square inch of the house into her own private little world. Piece by piece, household items and decorative little knickknacks that had been meaningful to my Camille were pushed aside and replaced by objects that were meaningful to my mother. To me, Camille existed in my heart—not in a collection of porcelain, glass, and metal decorative figurines. As long as I was able to maintain the Jennie-free zone behind my bedroom door, I didn't give a damn.

From time to time I hit the road and did what I had to do to pay the bills, but afterward, I always promptly returned home to my bed with an urn of Camille's ashes and my new best friend, Ketel One. My first show back was October 22nd at Foxwoods Casino, only five weeks after the funeral. I spent far too much of the act talking about Camille and bumming everyone out. You could hear the moans and groans from the audience. They weren't paying good money to get depressed. After two nights of converting the showroom into a morgue, I got back to my usual script and turned in a decent third show.

Still, too many of the shows from this period descended into a haze of boozy, distracted performances. Oh, I could still sing my ass off. Dick Fox always jokes with me that I'll still be able to sing when I have six feet of dirt piled on top of me. The shows suffered for non-vocal reasons. In one of them, I collapsed into a stagehand's arms as soon as I walked into the wings after taking my bows. Security had to take me back to my room in a wheelchair. A few weeks later, I went on stage in Florida all lit up and thought I'd delivered a great fifty-to-sixty minute set. The next day I found out it was closer to twenty minutes. The venue was really pissed.

When I finally got my ass out of the bedroom after a year, you could say that life came back. But the gigs didn't. Neither did sobriety. I was still hitting the bottle at a dangerous pace. As word got around, Dick started getting disturbing calls from booking agents who had kept me working over the years. I'd become a risky act to book. By 2007, the gigs had trickled down to next to nothing.

Dick really showed me something during those lean years. He never lectured me, and somehow still managed to be supportive. The same with Fabe and Frank. Let's face it: In spite of my being a total asshole more times than I'd like to remember—not to mention that my behavior was threatening the financial stability of the act—both of them hung in there with me. I don't want to minimize how big a test it all was for them. We had performed almost eight hundred concerts over the years; we'd played in front of presidents and huge crowds at stadiums like the Meadowlands. And here I was, doing everything I could to throw it all away.

I was no prize at this point in my life, so the logical question would seem to be, "Why would anyone have put up with me and my bullshit?" Who knows? Maybe it was a South Philly thing—a special bond between the three of us that came from growing up in the old neighborhood. All I know is, I would have never made it without them.

Dick Fox and me backstage at Caesars in Atlantic City.

Despite my best (or, I should probably say, "worst") efforts to wreck everything, the Golden Boys was still a great act.

At the urging of local DJ Don Cannon and some other friends, I took the next step and started getting out and about in Philadelphia. We all started a weekly routine of hitting a different South Philly Italian restaurant every Wednesday night. At one of those outings, I met a woman named Linda Hoffman—ironically, the same exact name of my fan club president Linda Ferrino since she'd married Jake Hoffman. The coincidences didn't just stop with their names: They knew each other and had the same dentist, hairdresser, and jeweler. We hit it off from the start. Linda was smart and independent. She had worked for over three decades in the medical field as a cardiac sonographer. Little did either of us realize how valuable that background would be in the next few years.

One of the things that attracted me to her the most was that she knew almost nothing about me or my career. She thought I was either dead or was the guy who sang "Mack the Knife," (who, being Bobby Darin, was also dead.) Our first official date was on Halloween 2007 at a Passyunk Avenue Italian eatery named Tre Scalini. I didn't give it much thought at the time, but it's such a perfectly appropriate description for what was going on in my life. "Tre Scalini" means "three little steps" in English. My first step had been leaving my bedroom; the second was getting out again among people; and now, the third step was entering into what would soon be a new, intimate relationship with a woman.

While my mother was happy that I was finally pulling out of my tailspin, she wasn't happy with the reason why. Linda was an immediate threat to her. Mom hadn't even wanted me to marry Camille. Still, as much as she may have wanted to forbid it, she had enough self-restraint to keep her mouth shut. Instead, she just bided her time. After the deaths of my dad and Camille, she finally had me all to herself. The last thing she wanted was to have to start sharing me again—especially with another female.

Aside from being pure hell, the four years in between Camille's passing and Linda's entrance were sometimes borderline creepy. On occasion, Mom would tell people I was her husband and sometimes referred to me as "Ott," my father's old nickname. I'd blow a gasket every time it happened, and then she'd always apologize and blame it on the dementia that was increasingly taking control of her mental faculties. She was probably ninety percent accurate about that being the reason why she said those things. The other ten percent? I don't even want to think about it.

As Linda and I saw each other more and more, I sometimes stayed overnight at her apartment. Mom would call a dozen times asking me when I was coming home, sometimes demanding to know if I was "out with that whore again." Linda was tough. She'd grab the phone and tell my mother that I was with her and I was fine; I'd come home when I felt like it, and she was just going to have to learn to deal with it.

The irony in all of this is that my mother had finally evolved into Mae, the crazy, meddlesome, widowed mother Maureen Stapleton played in *Bye Bye Birdie*. One of the film's subplots involved Mae's repeated attempts to sabotage her son Albert's relationship with his girlfriend Rosie, so she could have him all to herself. Sounds familiar, huh? Life imitating art.

Linda and I started vacationing in Caribbean island destinations like Cancun, San Juan, and Nassau. By that time, my mother was more or less out of the picture. Her dementia had progressed to the point where I had to put her in a nursing home. I'd visit her every week. She knew who I was, but was distant and mostly just stared into space. On January 7th, 2009, Mom passed away at the age of ninety-two from a combination of the dementia and congestive heart failure. I felt like ten thousand pounds had been lifted off my chest.

A few months before, I'd asked Linda if she wanted to live together with me and was told, "No. The only way I'll live with you is if we're married; otherwise we'll just continue dating."

With my mother in Wildwood a year before she passed away.

On January 17th, 2009, ten days after my mother's death, we got married at the Bootlegger Bistro in Las Vegas. Linda didn't have much of a grace period before the start of yet another round of bullshit and drama. She really had no idea how bad my drinking problem was, not because of naiveté on her part, but because I'd become a master in the art of concealment. I'd begun hiding full bottles of vodka in my golf bag and getting rid of the empty ones in dumpsters around the neighborhood.

Tying the knot with Linda in Las Vegas.

I did the worst damage to myself on the road when I knew I'd be out of Linda's sight. In spite of my gastroenterologist's late 2009 warning that I'd be dead within two years if I didn't stop drinking, I felt great through 2010 and the beginning of 2011. But in that year and a half, I was guilty of the worst behavior of my life. I'd actually defied the laws of physics and hit *below* rock bottom. I knew I had a problem, but in my warped thinking, I interpreted my doctor's warning as authorization to let it

In my usual state of denial, performing at Philadelphia's Clef Club.

all hang out and have a hell of a good time for two years before I checked out. Somehow, I pulled myself together for an important Time-Life video project filmed on April 1st, 2011 at Caesars in Atlantic City called *Malt Shop Memories*. A lot of my old friends were on the program—Frank and Fabe, Little Anthony and the Imperials, Lesley Gore, Lenny Welch, the Drifters, and a half-dozen other stars of the '50s and '60s. I did alright, but I looked and felt terrible.

As to how or why I continued to work through all this, I have no answers other than to credit my wife Linda and Dick Fox. The stability Linda brought to my life—outside of my drinking—enabled me to be somewhat functional. And I'd

Another Houdini-esque, escape artist routine: Don't ask me how, but I actually pulled off a decent performance on the Time-Life "Malt Shop Memories" show.

be remiss if I didn't credit Dick's managerial expertise for still being able to convince promoters to book me. I needed the income and I still loved performing, so I did what I could to deliver quality performances and keep up my end of the bargain. But the results were mixed. I was too far gone.

At a Golden Boys New Year's Eve date at the Borgata Casino in Atlantic City, my stomach was visibly distended. I sang OK, but just OK. Frank noticed and told Dave Kovnat, "This is one of the last shows he's gonna make. He looks like he's gonna die soon." A few days later, I was lying in bed and Linda commented that I looked like I was pregnant with quintuplets.

It wasn't from overeating; fluid was building up in my stomach—a medical condition called ascites. In the early months of 2012, I had to start going to the hospital at least once a week to get it tapped. I'd stopped drinking in January 2012, but not by choice. Linda put together an intervention composed of family members, some friends, Dick Fox, and a shrink. It had the desired effect; their arguments were all the more convincing due to the considerable amount of time I was spending in and out of the hospital. But it was really sobriety by default; hospitals usually don't let you drink vodka on the premises.

It didn't matter. By the time I quit, the horse had long since left the barn. Cirrhosis of the liver had begun to make it difficult for my body to cleanse itself of toxins. On one of my hospital visits to have my abdomen tapped, I could barely breathe when I arrived. The doctors drained almost twelve liters of fluid. They could have siphoned off the Delaware River and it wouldn't have mattered. Within days, my body was making more of whatever they took out, and I had to start the cycle all over again.

Like a sputtering old jalopy whose engine was about to seize up, my decades-long life of denial finally traveled its last mile at a North Jersey oldies show in New Brunswick. It was on March 3rd, nine days before I was supposed to hit the road for an Australian tour. My voice sounded great, but I was forgetting lyrics I'd sung for years, and my in-between-songs banter was all nonsense. A brain disorder known as encephalopathy set in. I alternated between bouts of fatigue and irritability, and my my speech became slurred. Linda had seen enough. Convinced I'd come back in a body bag, she told Dick to cancel the tour. It had gotten to the point where I needed some new body parts.

The encephalopathy continued to take its toll. During one of my hospital stays following the cancellation of the tour, I was angry with Linda and tried to say, "Aah, your sister's ass" but all that came out was, "Sassafrass." I was also hallucinating and calling for "Mommy." I say "hallucinating" because by now, you all know my mother would have been the last person in the world I would have wanted to see.

If any blessing came as a result of my health crises, it was that it helped heal a major rift between Robert Jr., Jennifer, and myself. The kids took Camille's death extremely hard. When she passed away, I told them I didn't think I would ever remarry. "No one could ever replace your mother," I explained. Six years later when I married Linda, they believed I'd gone back on my word—which I had. But of course, anyone who's lived through what I did knows it's not always that

Before the New Brunswick concert: I looked like death warmed over, and my stomach was very distended. I would have never have made it without Linda.

simple. Regardless, it didn't sit well with them. The situation wasn't helped by the embarrassment I caused them when I was arrested on a DUI charge during the same time period. I had smashed my car into a wall in Narberth, a small Philly suburb a few miles from my house. The kids and I didn't talk for several years.

The hardest part for me was not seeing my grandkids: Robert's two sons, Robert Vincent and Tristen, his daughter, Jayden, and Jennifer's son, Caden and daughter, Delaney. It was going to take a while to heal things. Eventually, Jennifer and Robert got wind of how sick I was. She showed up at the house on May 31st, and Robert followed a few weeks later. I didn't care what their reasons were for ending the feud; I was just happy and grateful we were back together as a family.

Jennifer, Robert, and me reunited.

Because of the severity of my condition, I was finally listed for a transplant on June 28th, 2012. The operation was shaping up to be quite a party. In May, both my kidneys failed and I started going for dialysis three times a week. The new liver I needed would now have to be accompanied by a date—a new kidney. The burning questions were: "Would these two organs be available in time," and "Would they be suitable matches?" The bill for immediate payment was now due on the two-year warning from my doctor; I only had a week or two to live. By July 8th, it looked like I was a goner. Lying in bed, I told Linda,

"You better start getting my papers in order. I don't think I'm gonna make it." She paid me no mind and stayed positive. "If there's a week for this to happen, this is the one," she said.

The next morning we got a call from Thomas Jefferson Hospital telling us a liver and a kidney had become available. It would only be a partial liver, and if I wanted it, I had to leave immediately to get prepped for surgery. Linda instantly turned to me and said, "Take it." It wasn't an optimal situation. I was splitting the liver with a little girl. Fourteen other people had rejected the offer of the partial, but I wasn't in a position to be choosy. The first person I called before leaving for the hospital was Frankie Avalon. He cried and then immediately headed to church to pray for me. There were times in both of our lives when we weren't that close. We had had our issues over the years, but the Golden Boys had brought us back together. After all the years of dumb arguments and my acting like an ass and pissing him off, I knew Cheech still loved me like a brother.

I arrived at the hospital on July 9th at 12:30 p.m. and by 3:00, I was in the operating room ready to undergo a twenty-hour procedure. The liver went in first and then the kidney. I spent three days in the intensive care unit, after which they transferred me to a regular hospital room. Dr. Doria and Dr. Ramirez, the surgeons who transplanted the organs, told me I'd be home in five to six days. Linda asked if they could keep me five to six weeks so *she* could recuperate. But with medical insurance guidelines currently being what they are, we both knew there was no chance of that.

Cheech got pissed at me countless times, but he never gave up on me.

As you can imagine, a giddy, celebratory mood swept through my hospital room in the wake of the operation's success. It was one big party for all my family members and friends who stopped by to visit. I felt it too, but in the down time when I was all alone, troubling questions poked through the fog of painkillers and post-op medications. Once again, I'd proven to be Houdini, surviving yet another close call that would have been curtains for most people. How many more times could I do that before my luck ran out? And would I recover enough to be able to sing again? But the most pressing question was: "Who was this person whose liver and kidney were now living inside of me?

⊕　⊕　⊕

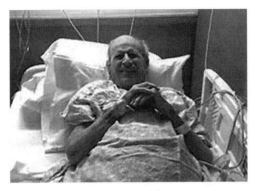

In intensive care, post-surgery.

Her name was Julia. She was a beautiful twenty-one-year-old girl who, tragically, had been hit by a car while crossing the street. She flew thirty-five feet in the air from the impact. They rushed her to the hospital, but due to massive head injuries, she was already brain-dead. Unbeknownst to her parents, Julia had previously signed on to be an organ donor. That decision saved seven other lives after she passed. When I finally met her family, there was a lot of tears and hugging. Emotions flew in all directions. We all mourned her loss, but her parents were happy that at least a part of her was going to live on.

As for me, my deepest feelings about Julia took a while to sort out. I was always a very emotional person. I never felt the need to put up a phony macho front. If I felt like crying, I just cried and didn't give a damn who saw it. Since my transplant surgery, the tears come more frequently—actually, a lot more frequently. You could say I cry at the drop of a hat. Maybe it's just a side effect of the surgery. I think it may be because there's a piece of Julia in me now and I'm in touch with my feminine side. If that makes me feel closer to her and to my new life, then that's OK.

But what would that life be like now? As a result of my prolonged illness, the surgery, and then the time spent recuperating, I'd just gone through the longest period of downtime from singing and performing since I was an infant in the crib. There was a black hole of nothingness in my soul that needed to be filled by a song—not just one that I could *hear*, but one that I could *sing*. It was plain and simple: If I couldn't sing, there was no me.

Now I had a new fear to deal with. Oh, I probably could have carried a tune five minutes after I woke up in the intensive care ward. But that's not what I'm talking about. I'm talking about *singing*—singing all out, the way I'd done it my entire life. A few months after I came home, I invited my old drummer Joe Nero, bassist Craig Thomas, and guitarist Al Slutsky to come over to my house and play through a few tunes with me. They told me I sounded great. I knew better; I couldn't sustain a note. I got very little sleep that night. All my life, I'd smoked like a fiend, but in spite of that, every note I ever sang always came out—Pow!!—big as can be. Was I finally paying the piper for all those years of abusing my lungs, or was this vocal deficiency from the surgery?

In late September, I gave it another shot at Philadelphia's Clef Club with my old buddy Lou Cioci and the Monday night rehearsal band. We played through some of the charts from my show repertoire, and with each new tune, my voice came back a little stronger. By the end of the evening, everything was there except the stamina. I was out of breath, but greatly encouraged.

A month later, I kept my pre-operating room promise to Linda: I made the *Malt Shop Memories Cruise*. It was a non-paying gig. I couldn't possibly sing a full show yet, but the cruise line was kind enough to fly Linda and me down to meet the ship in San Juan, Puerto Rico. I went onstage with Frankie Avalon and Jerry Blavat and sang one song: "Mack the Knife." The audience—fully aware that I'd just come back from major surgery—gave me a warm welcome and a tremendous, heartwarming ovation after the tune.

Still, my comeback trail was a work in progress. The next thing on the agenda was to work on my confidence. Not yet trusting my chops when I was asked to sing at a high rollers' Christmas party at the Borgata, I asked Al Slutsky to lower the keys on a couple of songs. Leaving the stage after sounding like Melvin Franklin of the Temptations, I laughed and said, "Uh, guess I shoulda stayed in the original key, huh?" But I hadn't learned my lesson yet. I did the same exact thing a few weeks later, lowering the key of "The Lady Is a Tramp" at an Italian Festival in the Bronx. This time, I sounded like a 45 of Sinatra that had been set on 33 and 1/3 rpm.

So it was original keys or nothin'. I'd know soon enough if I was ready for it. My first real gig was as a solo artist—no Golden Boys to pick up my slack. It was in January 2013 on Linda's and my fourth wedding anniversary. I was back

Back in the saddle in January 2013 at the Sun Coast Casino in Las Vegas.

in Vegas playing the Sun Coast Casino for three nights. Remember how I bragged over and over that I never had stage fright? Well I sure as hell did on this particular opening night. I was extremely nervous, but my swagger quickly came back. Each of the three shows sold out and they wound up adding tables for the overflow. My voice was there; the audience was with me from the first note; life was good once again—but only for two months.

In March 2013, I failed a stress test and had double heart-bypass surgery a few days later. You probably think I'm messin' with you, but I'm not. I really did have the bypass surgery! Yet, in spite of it, life was still good. I mean, let's get real; after what I'd been through earlier in the year, the heart surgery was like a paper cut. I hadn't been feeling great before the procedure so Linda insisted I see a cardiologist right away. The cardiac catheterization he ordered showed a ninety to ninety-five percent blockage in one artery and seventy percent in the other. I had a booking to play Biloxi, Mississippi, but the doctor told me, "You aren't going anywhere." A few days later, no post-heart surgery depression, no shortness of breath, nothin'. Just some soreness from the surgical staples. I'd evolved into the bionic man of the showroom circuit. Within six weeks I was headlining at the sold-out Keswick Theater in Glenside, Pennsylvania.

So now it's Labor Day 2013, and here I am in the middle of three sold-out nights at the Atlantic Club Casino's showroom. I'm armed with some new charts and I'm prowling the stage like a hungry tiger. The Mike Natale Orchestra is kicking ass all over the house and taking no prisoners, and I have two thousand friends in the audience partying with me each night as I sing "Volare." I could do no wrong.

For the time being, it feels like Atlantic City back in its heyday. We're a lot alike, me and A.C. We've taken a lot of hits in recent years but we're still standing and doin' our thing.

Oh, and by the way, You!—the guy in the third row who had the big mouth at the beginning of this book. Yeah, you—the gavone with the *"Yo Bobby, I got your biography right hee-ah!"* Well, Pal, you're right; you do have my biography *"right hee-ah."* Thanks for taking the journey with me all these years.

CODA

"The sun shines out of your ass, Bob."

After three decades of conducting and playing drums for me—not to mention his being a musical soulmate and my close buddy through all my ups and downs—you'd figure Dave Kovnat might sum up my life with a slightly more elegant choice of words. But after having survived double transplant and heart surgeries and going through the introspective process of writing this autobiography, it's hard for me to argue with his summation of my life.

After reading these few hundred pages of my story, you know by now that I experienced the same assortment of bad and unlucky things that most people go through during their lifetimes: Camille died at a relatively young age; I didn't always have the greatest relationships with my kids; and God knows, I could have had a more supportive and loving mother. But more often than not, I was the ultimate escape artist. For every bad choice or mistake I've made throughout my seventy-three years, someone has always stepped forward to bail my butt out.

Sometimes it was a Bernie Lowe who said "Yes" when every other record label said "No"; there was always a Louie "D" or an Angelo Bruno who stepped in when I screwed up and was in over my head; and I'd be ungrateful if I failed to mention the nightclub owners and promoters who were willing to give me a second chance and still believed in my talent—even after my drinking problems made me a risky act to book. And finally, there was an angel named Julia whose ill-fated death gave me a second shot at life.

I have no idea how to process all this. I'm not a philosopher and I'm definitely not a psychiatrist. I don't know if I should feel guilty, unworthy, or just accept the hand I've been dealt and be happy and grateful for my abundance of good fortune. But, if it's possible to look someone in the eye through a printed page and be deadly honest, I have to tell you this: The only truth I've ever known is the music. The gift I was given some seven decades ago has brought me a level of financial security and fame beyond the comprehension of most people. But I don't think that's why I was put here.

In the end, I've come to realize that the only difference my life has made in this world is that I've been able to bring joy to millions of people through my jokes and impersonations, my acting, and most of all, my voice. Continuing down that path with a new sense of purpose and appreciation may not be the most profound answer to the questions I've posed to myself, but helping to bring a little light into this world isn't a bad place to start.

See you all at the next downbeat . . .

𝄞 A FEW MORE
(FOR THE ROAD)

I've always been a huge sports fan. From left to right: Mike Goffredo of the South Philly Review, *Philadelphia Eagles legend Chuck Bednarik, toothpick-sized me, middleweight world boxing champ, Joey Giardello, world heavyweight champ, Rocky Marciano, and Eagles wide receiver and tight end, Pete Retzlaff.*

Ronnie Linde surrounded by my albums and 45s. Ronnie was the chapter president of the Franklin Square, New York Bobby Rydell fan club. Kudos to Frankie Day and Linda Ferrino for putting together such a wide-ranging national fan network. I still have no idea how they did it.

A Cameo-era concert in Palisades Park, New Jersey.

Me and Annette Funicello.

Dave Kovnat, my drummer, conductor, and close friend for the last four decades.

Carl Mottola, Frankie Day, and I took a day trip to meet Harry Truman in his Independence, Missouri office. I was appearing that week at the Starlight Theater in nearby Kansas City.

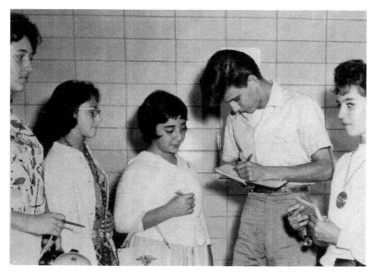

Signing autographs for fans in Utica, New York, sometime in 1962.

*A typical page from one of the dozens of teen magazines
that featured articles on me in the early-to-mid-'60s.*

Were Cheech and I ever really that young?

Playing to a packed house. The Fender Stratocaster neck combined with the black and white photography really gives this shot a cool, early rock and roll look.

With my parents, at one of my many shows at Sciolla's.

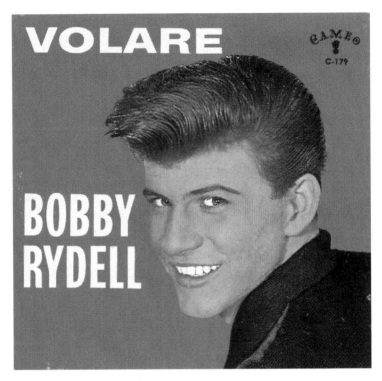

The record that provided me with the melody I've used behind my entrances and exits from the stage for over fifty years.

DISCOGRAPHY

SINGLES

1958 Fatty Fatty/ Happy Happy (Venise 201)

1958 Fatty Fatty/ Dream Age (Veko 731)

1959 Please Don't Be Mad/ Makin' Time (Cameo 160)

1959 All I Want Is You/ For You For You (Cameo 164)

1959 Kissin' Time/ You'll Never Tame Me (Cameo 167)

1959 We Got Love/ I Dig Girls (Cameo 169)

1960 Wild One/ Little Bitty Girl (Cameo 171)

1960 Swingin' School/ Ding A Ling (Cameo 175)

1960 Volare/ I'd Do It Again (Cameo 179)

1960 Sway/ Groovy Tonight (Cameo 182)

1961 Good Time Baby/ Cherie (Cameo 186)

1961 That Old Black Magic/ Don't Be Afraid (Cameo 190)

1961 The Fish/ The Third House (Cameo 192)

1961 I Wanna Thank You/ The Door To Paradise (Cameo 201)

BOBBY RYDELL

1962 I've Got Bonnie/ Lose Her (Cameo 209)

1962 I'll Never Dance Again/ Gee It's Wonderful (Cameo 217)

1962 The Cha-Cha-Cha/ The Best Man Cried (Cameo 228)

1963 Butterfly Baby/ Love Is Blind (Cameo 242)

1963 Wildwood Days/ Will You Be My Baby (Cameo 252)

1963 Little Queenie/ The Woodpecker Song (Cameo 265)

1963 Let's Make Love Tonight/ Childhood Sweetheart (Cameo 272)

1963 Forget Him/ Love, Love, Go Away (Cameo 280)

1964 Make Me Forget/ Little Girl You've Had A Busy Day (Cameo 309)

1964 A World Without Love/ Our Faded Love (Cameo 320)

1964 Ciao, Ciao, Bambino/ Voce De La Notte (Cameo 361)

1963 Steel Pier (one sided DJ) (Cameo 18E)

1964 I Just Can't Say Goodbye/ Two Is The Loneliest Number (Capitol 5305)

1965 Diana/ Stranger In The World (Capitol 5352)

1965 Sideshow/ The Joker (Capitol 5436)

1965 It Takes Two/ When I See That Girl Of Mine (Capitol 5513)

1965 Roses In The Snow/ The Word For Today (Capitol 5556)

1966 She Was The Girl/ Not You (Capitol 5696)

1966 You Gotta Enjoy Joy/ Open For Business As Usual (Capitol 5780)

1968 The Lovin' Things/ That's What I Call Livin' (Reprise 0656)

1968 The River Is Wide/ Absence Makes The Heart Grow Fonder (Reprise 0684)

1968 Every Little Bit Hurts/ Time And Changes (Reprise 0751)

1970 Chapel On The Hill/ It Must Be Love (RCA 47-9892)

1974 California Sunshine/ Honey Buns (Perception 519)

1974 Everything Seemed Better/ Sunday Son (Perception 552)

1976 Sway/ Sway (disco) (Pickwick 6515)

1976 Give Me Your Answer/ You're Not The Girl For Me (Pickwick 6521)

1976 The Single Scene/ It's Getting Better (Pickwick 6531)

BOBBY RYDELL

SINGLES RECORDED WITH CHUBBY CHECKER

1961 Your Hits And Mine (One Sided) (Cameo 12E)

1961 What Are You Doing New Year's Eve (One sided) (Cameo 13E)

1961 Jingle Bell Rock/Jingle Bell Imitations (Cameo 205)

1962 Swingin' Together/Teach Me To Twist (Cameo 214)

ALBUMS

1959 We Got Love Cameo (C-1006)

1960 Bobby Sings, Bobby Swings (Cameo C-1007)

1961 Biggest Hits (Cameo C-1009)

1961 Bobby Salutes the Great Ones (Cameo C-1010)

1961 Rydell At The Copa (Cameo C-1011)

1962 All The Hits (Cameo C-1019)

1962 Biggest Hits, Volume 2 (Cameo C-1028)

1962 An Era Reborn (Cameo C-4017)

1963 All The Hits, Volume 2 (Cameo C-1040)

1963 Bye Bye Birdie (Cameo C-1043)

1963 Wildwood Days (Cameo C-1055)

1964 The Top Hits of '63 (Cameo C-1070)

1964 Forget Him (Cameo C-1080)

1965 16 Golden Hits (Cameo C-2001)

1965 Somebody Loves You (Capitol T-2281)

1976 Born With A Smile (Pickwick 6818)

1983 At His Best, Today And Yesterday (Applause 1021)

1993 The Bobby Rydell Story - A Musical Journey (Regal Collectable Classics)

1995 The Best of Bobby Rydell (K-Tel 3378-2)

1998 Born With A Smile (Plum) Re-issued

ALBUMS RECORDED WITH CHUBBY CHECKER

1961 BOBBY RYDELL / Chubby Checker (Cameo C-1013)

1963 BOBBY RYDELL & Chubby Checker (Cameo C-1063)

ALBUMS RELEASED ON CD

1998 Born With A Smile

2000 Now & Then (R.D.R. Records)

2001 Complete Bobby Rydell (Capitol Records)

2003 A Philadelphia Christmas - BCI Eclipse

2005 The Best of Bobby Rydell - ABKCO Records

2010 Rydell at the Copa (re-released in stereo/digital remaster from circa 1960 work) ABKCO Records

2010 Bobby Rydell Salutes the Great Ones (re-released in stereo/digital remaster from circa 1960 work) ABKCO Records

ON TV

(Many of the following shows involved repeat appearances)

1952 *Paul Whiteman's TV Teen Club*

1959 *American Bandstand*

1960 *Make Room for Daddy* (with Danny Thomas)

1960 *The Perry Como Show*

1960 *The Jack Benny Show*

1960 *Rock-a-bye-the Infantry* (TV Pilot with William Bendix)

1961 *The Ed Sullivan Show*

1962 *Disney After Dark* (with Annette Funicello)

1962 *The Joey Bishop Show*

1962 *Swingin' Together* (TV Pilot with Stephanie Powers)

1962-1965 *The Red Skelton Hour*

1964 *Combat!* (with Vic Morrow)

1964 *The Milton Berle Show*

1964 *Where The Action Is* (TV Pilot)

1964-1965 *Shindig*

BOBBY RYDELL

1964-1968 *The Mike Douglas Show*

1965 *Hullaballoo*

1967 *Piccadilly Place*

1978 *Sha Na Na*

1985 *Live from Wolf Trap (PBS Special featuring the Golden Boys)*

1986 *Liberty Celebration* (National TV Special)

1987 *The Facts of Life*

1987 *The Whitehouse Farewell to President Reagan*

1990 *My Two Dads* (with Paul Reiser)

1993 *The Joan Rivers Show*

1993 *Live with Regis & Kathie Lee*

1994 *American Bandstand-33 1/3 Years*

FILMOGRAPHY

1960 *Swingin' School (Featured vocals on the soundtrack)*

1963 *Bye Bye Birdie (Columbia Pictures)*

1972 *Marco Polo Jr. (Australian animated cartoon with Bobby's voice)*

1973 *The Adventures of Marco Polo Jr. (Australian animated cartoon with Bobby's voice)*

1975 *That Lady from Peking*

1999 *Mr. Rock & Roll: The Alan Freed Story* (Made for TV Movie/NBC)

ACKNOWLEDGMENTS

From Bobby:

Without the help and friendship of all the people listed below, I'd still be playing stickball on the streets of South Philly (which wouldn't be such a bad thing). But here goes:

Thanks to Frankie Day, my first manager who always believed in me, and to Dick Fox, my present manager who created and conceived *The Golden Boys*. His loyalty through thick and thin has been invaluable and much appreciated. To Frankie (Cheech) Avalon and Fabian (Fabe) Forte—my fellow Golden Boys, and to Bernie Lowe, Kal Mann, and Dave Appell—the Cameo guys who produced and wrote my first hits. Thanks also to Cameo's master engineer, Joe Tarsia.

I can never forget Dick Clark, who gave me my first network TV appearance and supported my career through the years, and to all the DJs who played my records throughout my career. My debut at the Copacabana would have flopped if Lou Spencer and Noel Sherman hadn't done such a great job staging my nightclub act, and if not for George Sidney, I never would have had the chance to play Hugo Peabody in *Bye Bye Birdie*. Lot's of love to Onna White, *Bye Bye Birdie's* choreographer, who taught me all the moves while she was on crutches!! And to Ann-Margret, my Kim, and my close friend over the years.

Thanks to the teachers of my youth, vocal coach Artie Singer and Sam D'Amico, my first (and only) drum teacher, and to Marty Lawrence (The Professor), who saved my voice in just one lesson! A deep debt of gratitude to the singers and musicians who have mentored and inspired me, especially Frank Sinatra, Steve Lawrence, Bobby Darin, and Buddy Rich.

To the musicians who have worked and traveled with me throughout my career, I'd like to thank: Rocky Valentine, my classy conductor for eight years, and Joe Zito, who arranged and conducted my debut Copa show. I have a special place in my heart for my past drummers: Ray Deeley, Carl "Cochise" Mottola, Roger Ryan, Joe Nero, Jimmy Paxson, and Danny Gottlieb, and especially my current drummer and conductor, Dave Kovnat.

Thank you Evan Solot, Mike Pedicin, Jr., and George Mesterhazy for your work on my album *Now and Then,* and to Bill Zaccagni and Allan Slutsky for their great musical arrangements. My unending gratitude to the great players I have worked with through the years, whose stellar musicianship made me sound like a million bucks.

To all the loyal fans who have supported me through the years, you have my eternal love and gratitude, especially Linda Ferrino (Hoffman), who has been along for the entire bumpy career ride and has never lost faith. Without all of you, my long career would not have been possible.

To my childhood friends Lou Cioci, Joe Priori, Dave Piscatelli, and Pat (Azzara) Martino, thank you for being a part of my life and for letting me be a part of yours.

I'd be nothing without my family: my son Robert and his children, Robert, Tristen, and Jayden, my daughter Jennifer, her husband Jason, and their children, Caden and Delaney, my cousin Jody Sapienza and Dawne McHugh, and to my wife Linda J. Hoffman (Ridarelli), whose love and support got me through my darkest hours.

I wouldn't be here today if not for the care and skills of Thomas Jefferson Hospital surgeons Cataldo Doria, M.D. and Carlos Ramirez, M.D., and all staff who made my second chance possible. To my organ donor JULIA—you are my angel. And lastly, to Father Joseph Sica ("America's Guest"), whose spiritual guidance has inspired me throughout my adult years.

And to anyone I may have forgotten, it doesn't mean I don't love you. It just means I'm seventy-four and can't remember! So please forgive me and know I'm grateful you were in my life.

From Allan Slutsky:

I'd like to thank and acknowledge my writing heroes from the world of music journalism and music books: Susan Whitall, Adam White, Dave Marsh, David Ritz, Nelson George, and Fred Goodman—from whom I shamelessly steal turns of phrases, Michael Pedicin for hiring me on my first Bobby Rydell gig, my brilliant editor Ruth Fecych, to Harry

Weinger of Universal Records for teaching me to write concisely (even though I still have trouble doing it), and to Robert and Richard Adler, for allowing me to torment them by bouncing ideas off their heads at all hours of the day.

Much love to my departed big brother, Carl Mottola (Bobby's drummer through his early glory years), to Dave Kovnat (Bobby's conductor and drummer for the last four decades), thanks to Linda Ferrino (Hoffman) for all her help tracking down photos, and my eternal gratitude to my sister Joanne Slutsky for additional editing help and to her husband, Joseph Valente, for his invaluable writing advice. And lastly, to my three sons Daniel, Sammy, and Michael, and especially my wife Rachel: Thank you for still loving me—and putting up with me—as I go about my assorted musical crusades.

ALLAN SLUTSKY is a Grammy Award-winning musician, arranger, and film and record producer, who is known to guitarists as "Dr. Licks," for his series of guitar transcription books. His previous books include *The Funkmasters: The Great James Brown Rhythm Sections 1960-1973* and *Standing In The Shadows of Motown,* which won the 1989 *Rolling Stone*–BMI Ralph J. Gleason Award for music book of the year and was released as a feature film in 2002. Based in Philadelphia, Allan has played guitar behind Bobby Rydell on numerous occasions since they first met in 1992.